AFTER

Peter Weltner

ISBN: 979-8-218-41923-3

McAdoo Farm and Battenkill were previously published in Vespers on Point Reyes: Selected Poems 1989-2019, BrickHouse Books (Baltimore), edited by Clarinda Harriss.

Reverberations, Marlowe's Passion, and After Sinkei and Wang Wei (as Sage) were previously published in Crow-Black Stones and a Flock of Crows, Agenda Editions (UK), edited by Patricia McCarthy.

The two photos of Gerald Coble accompanying Reverberations were taken by Dana Nunnelley, niece of Gerald's partner for sixty years, the artist Robert Nunnelley.

Except for the scrapbook of pictures in Book II, Part II, all the other images included in it, whether drawing, sculpture, painting, or assemblage, are by Gerald Coble, work made from the late fifties or early sixties to late in his life.

The majority of Gerald Coble's work included in this book is untitled except for a few of the pieces Gerald called "Small Monuments" whose titles appear on the base of the sculpture and these other images: Sicilian Door, 41, Elba, 57, August 1st, 76, August 2nd, 77, Carolina Field, 92 and 93.

In descending order, the photographs on 137 are of the Battenkill, Laguna Beach, and three of Ocean Beach, San Francisco.

I want to thank Galen Garwood for all he has given me through the years—inspiration, encouragement, friendship, the genius of his kindness and understanding, the goodness of his heart, the intensity and originality of his vision and of his art. We have collaborated often during the last decade and longer. Nothing means more to me than what he has shown me through his eye and spirit.

AFTER

Peter Weltner

Sculpture, Paintings, Assemblages, Drawings
Gerald Coble (1932-2021)

For
Atticus Carr and Robert Mohr
and in memory of
Robert Colley and John Nichols

marrowstone press

Table of Contents

Book II

Part I

BOOK I

Part I

Rhyming Blues for John Nichols

A flawed, slightly cracked, thick aquamarine glass goblet
sits on my living room's mantle as if waiting
for the sun each morning to spill into it, flow through it,
tinting two chalk-white walls and the plaster ceiling a cloudless sky blue.

When I was young, in the Bahamas, I watched a man wade into
water that was a serene turquoise and stab and spear
black sea porcupines he threw into a burlap sack. The slaughter
turned the sea's calm blue to a burning scarlet the ebbing tide would
quickly clear.

Naked except for loose boxer shorts that uncannily shine with the same
blue as his irises, Nick strums
a guitar in his dorm room and hums
to the tune. He's chipped a front tooth in a hockey game.
Strands of his curly, yellow hair flop over his eyes,
blue as a pool's water, too,
                or Jarman's blinded blue
                            or the blue of Hiroshige's stormy skies.

The Magic Journey

Half buried in sand, slivers and bits of bones glisten, sun-
bleached fragments broken by battering
winds, scattered by relentless winter rains and sudden flooding.

A sad, funny, meandering novel is stacked in a bookcase unread,
yellowing, foxing, waiting for someone to open
it again, to celebrate, laugh, cry for lost lives, mourning their own dead.

Suppose words could be found hiding in spring meadows, beside an arroyo,
among scrub pine roots: a thimble, a cigarette butt, hawks' feathers,
bullets' casings, a needleless compass, a tarnished key, dried flowers,

columbine, poppies, Apache plumes. Then imagine a man after life's end
walking alone by morning, finding waiting for him in desert sands
near his old adobe a pottery shard he holds up to read like a long lost book in his hands.

Desert Moon

Not mythological. Nothing mystical to plumb.
No metaphysical resistance to penetrate.
A full moon over a desert, the sand white-

water-white, an ungraspable purity to it,
bleaching agave, yucca, cacti, mesquite
to white, seeping through branches of ironwood,

Joshua trees' bristling branches. Moonlight
thick as morning fog, chilly as mist. A moon
for us to plunge into like cold water. A shining

impossible to hold on to or keep. So we praise it,
even if we do not want to, sensing desolation
in it, its insistence on silence, its ancient intimations

of catastrophe and painful joys. A brilliant moon,
sagacious, resplendent, its lunar light protective,
yet inhumane, illuminating the prophesied end: the red

of the mesa in the shape of an amphitheater,
whose echoing ghosts I heard and saw with you
greeting us together one night near Abiquiu, New Mexico.

After Fragments of Alkaios

Imagine a boy slyly spying on another boy on Lesbos
as he pleads to the sea to bring back
his lover from foreign wars.   A horned grebe
flies over a grove of olive trees. A boat

heading for harbor leaps waves like a dolphin.
The boy wades into the lapping water. Loss
has half-crazed him. Nearby, fishermen stack
their flapping catch on the dock. A flayed goat

skin hangs drying in a doorway. It is a golden,
sundering summer morning, thunder sounding
over mountains, though no rain falls, wells
run dry, and parched mouths drink cheap wine

to quench a thirst, never satisfying what they need.
The boy weeps as he weeps at beauty, what it tells
him of mortality, the bitter taste of tears like brine
in the wind. A hobbled woman in a black shawl wails

at the sight of him for no reason. He turns round. The other
boy waves like a stranger. You and I, remember?,
met like that. I mean in some intensity of grief you'd
never lose, no matter how much we loved one another.

I learned this lesson from reading fragments of poems,
otherwise lost, in the Greek Anthology, often just bits
and pieces surviving the ruins of time: how one roams
through it seeking one's life, images from the past that fit it.

I listen as Alkaios says, Quench your thirst with wine. The dog star
wheels in the sky, bringing back summer. Sweet
in the leaves, cicadas cry. Come home to me.   Artichokes are
in flower.   And men's passions swell, surge free, wanton as the sea or summer's heat.

Pan

1.

Sunshine in an open doorway, his hair like downy feathers,
like a horse's mane whipping in the wind. Standing
out of the light, in the shadows of a cavernous
hall, he summons from the shade a sprawling garden,
scrub shrubs sculpted like a topiary's. The weather's
splendid, the air blossoming, apple trees, dogwood growing
toward glory. It's a morning, he thinks, belonging to us,
his and his friend's, not lost, never over, no more forbidden,
no naked, sad boy, ripe as day, bidding good-bye
while the wind blows fiercely, looking west, far away,
wondering what awaits him years ahead in a distant city.
No, only him and Paul, why not call him Paul?, two boys at play
at sunset stepping out of a pool or a lake or the sea,
drying each other with towels still warm from lying in
the sun all afternoon. So what if an old man's best life is only
a child's fantasy? Reality is unbearable. Let him dream. Let him see it
clearly.

2.

Waves rock him sleeplessly
to sleep. His is the city
of old age,
destitute of visitations.

Nearby is the port he sought.
the sea-lanes
he'd sail
before his life is lost.

Dream-bearer of tides,
of oceans,
urn-carrier,
keep by him, assure him

he'll not die like his progenitor
alone,
half-mad,
and wanting water.

3.

A man stands alone on a dune. The beach this morning's
been battered by storms. It's low tide. The sea
is yellow by force of dawn, the sand appearing
to stretch all the way to the horizon, an illusory
sign of an endless desert, the dead he must remember
or lose forever. His past feels like dreams he's jotted
down in a notebook he cannot bear to read for fear
they will make no sense any more, now his allotted
time is nearly over. How little he recalls, how much forgotten.
It is not regret he feels, perhaps, as something stranger.
Sometimes it takes a fable to change him. The land of Eden
is a forsaken place. There's a boy on a rock playing a pipe
to sunrise. The old, foolish man imagines he's a pagan
of a hippie kind, loved by Pan, young and joyous and ripe
with life. So what if it's nonsense, the beautiful sadness, the madness,
he feels inside him from envy of the children making their own world,
remembering nothing?

4.

What if the beauty of the universe were to be at last spent
not as violently as it was created,
but out of exhaustion as if a final sleep were all it had meant?

Near a broken oak tree, rotting, splintered,
a flock of starlings preens on the grass, black,
white-spotted, opalescent, lovely in the setting sun.

The western park is evening quiet, though fragmented
by the coming of darkness. The man stands back
to hear them sing, the others following after the first one

started its song, melodic, tuneful, gentle, sweet,
so simple he could whistle it, too, as if to recall
long ago a boy whistling to him, sweeping him off his feet.

And then suddenly the flock flew off and that was the glorious all
of it, not exactly an epiphany, too much an attack
of panic to it, the beauty of things, like starlings flying away,

made ecstatic by vanishing, like memories dying, since nothing can stay,
and he and the boy lolling on the lawn, dozing, dreaming till
the sun boldly reddens in a twilight perpetually ending in that springtime still.

Xenios

Given the choice by my own plaited haired sea-goddess
mother between a long life and a short one of fame
and glory, afraid of becoming too soon bodiless bat-
squeak hanging upside down in a dank cave by an icy sea,

I chose to live until the raging storms of age felled me, a leafless
tree among many like it in a withering wilderness. Stranger, you
who read this rough-hewn block of stone, remember me, say
the name of one who never knew a day of fame, never tasted immortal glory.

After Reading Simone Weil on the Poem of Force

Imagine yourself in Athens at the Theater
of Dionysos during the spring or the fall
festival in the fifth century before the coming
of Christ at a performance of Antigone
while she chants her last speech, her threnody
to life. Think of yourself at a rite like that,
what it means for your time, your city, and its
people should you fail to listen, to heed her warnings.

Or see yourself in Troy as a man and his sons
are trapped, coiled by snakes attacking them
from holes they slithered out of, the wet-hemp-
like-noose of serpents strangling them. Consider
the father's, his sons' terror at being suffocated,
struggling to free, save themselves from the scaly
knots shackling, ensnaring them, taking their
lives, crushing them, smothered, asphyxiated:
the sons as doomed by the sea-god as their father,
a priest who saw the future too clearly, who dared
to warn of the trick of the horse and was not believed.

Who would you be, watching them die, heaving a cry,
bellowing like bulls being led to the altar while the city
behind them, its ancient walls and towers, is being
destroyed, set on fire? Bored gods, indifferently
gazing down? Incredulous, horrified Trojans?
Grinning Greeks cheering it on, the sacrifice, the deaths,
the slaughter? Or would you wonder, like a doomed-to-die
Antigone moments before her entombment why piety dooms the faithful to suffer?

Livia Drusilla

Flowers still bloom on Capri like pre-Raphaelite women
with fantastical heads of hair, mortal as sirens'
tresses, the smell of the sea in the air, the sun
each day entering dramatically, moorhens
preening, peacocks displaying their fans. It all
looks shot through the lens of an ardent, love-sick
photographer with a dandy's fancy eye, a villa
whose gardens are lush but not formal, thick,
entangled with vines and ivy, a Tiberian floral
paradise where the thorn is more honored than
the rose, as if aware how lovers linger far longer
in their graves than in bed. Imagine some Cleopatra
captured here in each petal's rapt colors, its kiss
more poisonous, fatal than hers. Tell me, then, Livia
Drusilla, which did you choose to kill Augustus? Datura,
belladonna, hemlock? How sensual and devious history is.

Crabbing

It is late at night, shortly before dawn. The tide
is at its lowest, the waves rumbling, grumbling,
roaring like a long line of distant trucks moving
slowly down a highway toward a town or village

during a war. In their hip-high waders, crabbers
scan the shoreline with their flashlights for crabs
left on the sand by the retreating sea. The hunt
looks sometimes like faraway floodlights searching

for planes hidden by clouds. During a mescaline trip,
a young Jean-Paul Sartre grew terrified of crustaceans.
All his life, he feared a giant lobster would catch
him in its claws. How does one tell the difference

between horror and comic irony? The crabbers pick up
the flailing crabs with gloved hands and toss them
in their pails. Tonight, they'll steam some, crack their shells,
and eat their sweet, succulent flesh, satisfying their hunger, thinking nothing of it.

The Named and Nameless Fallen

1.

Rescued after centuries of lying at the bottom
of the sea, a statue rises nobly again on
a plinth in the city's museum's largest room
devoted to antiquities, erect as a column
from a temple, a tall marble kouros, solemn
as a priest might be worshiping in a sacred place.

Beside it rests a carved olive wood figure
of a boy that's survived centuries with only a trace
of gold substituting for his eyes.
                          Outside, the weather
is inclement, the sea dark as grape pulp
or the dregs from a wine cup. Imagine a ship,
ram-headed, dolphin-eyed while hungry gulls
circle above it as it heads to Sicily for a last trip,
headed for disaster, the ruin of Athens' greatness and all
the wars and deaths and betrayals that will follow
Alcibiades wherever he goes until enemies' arrows
pierce his aging, ambitious soldier's body.
                          Now ask yourself what is Greece
to you today, millennia after, if it never knew peace
or its enduring solace but only tragedy and its repetitive sorrows.

2.

Remember how Philoctetes lived on an island meant for the solitary,
a man abandoned because of his wound,
its stinking, foul suppurations. A lonely sea
surrounded him and his cave, with only the sound
of waves and the cry of birds to comfort

him, no way to go home or get help, his foot bound
by bandages, oozing with blood and fetid pus.
He is a man of the earth and its sufferings, bored
by time, ruined by destiny's furies.
                                    He is us,
who stare at him as he hides in his wind-worn cave
torn from jagged cliffs and rock. No friends, kin,
lovers seek to aid him. Only his bow can save
him with its Herculean power to destroy Troy
forever.

And we in our technological world, though the rout
of that doomed city is long over, forgotten, do we not wonder
why tyrants and warriors still seek his bow to employ
its magical power to kill and so be victorious?
                              What if it were better to suffer
like Philoctetes in his cave, too canny to be tricked, and thereby spared their victory?

3.

In a documentary about '22, the docks are packed with pets,
livestock, boxes, people. The nights are frantic. The sun
as it rises bleeds into the sea. You hear gunshots
close by, meant to terrify you. No one Greek gets
to stay. The boat they're to leave on is set upon
by Turks, Ilium's revenge, while body after body rots
on the deck.
                  The skiff passes Chios. It seems
to say violence arrives to satisfy humanity's dreams
of retribution. Goats nibble on thistles, weeds. A church
rings its tower's bells in consolation. The churning water

the exiles travel on steams from the heat. Their throats
are parched, hands and feet blistered.
                              Decades later, some search
the plains, the mountains they've been forced out of by war,
hunt for bones, teeth, clothes, relics, anything from a grave
that might speak to who they were, that might save
a few memories.
                    In Plato's Apology, Socrates, lifelong gadfly
and ironist, shortly before he was doomed by the democracy to die,
offered a cock to Asclepius as if that gift might suffice to justify the tragedy.

4.

Pretend this, then, is also true. A boy watches the sea by Naxos, young
as the god he prays to
as he hums to his lord a song sung
to him by his mother. You,
too, would weep before
such beauty with your stranger's tears,
condemn, abhor
his wasted years as you do your youthful own.
                                        You cruise the piers.
A horned grebe flies over an olive tree's
branches. A fisherman's boat
leaps waves like a dolphin. A flayed goat
skin dries in the hot, whistling breezes.
                              It is Greece,
ancient Greece, you say to yourself pondering
the story, the terror and wonder
of Pentheus' folly, like that of the god, one sundering summer,
who maddened you, confusing you into believing
tragedy could offer you, if you truly adored him, a peace
more lasting and real than history's meager, famine-improverished offerings.

5.

Some Greeks believed the phenomenon of languages
began in mourning, in ululations that
made it possible to understand

what grief is. Who does not desire to live
longer than a generations' old olive
tree, to write a poem that might survive

you, like a marble shard,
firm and hard
to the grip, you've stolen and casually pocketed?

Stone walls.
Ancient halls
No matter what, the city falls.

I know little more
than it remains fitting for those alive to pour
wine on graves, to grieve for all the named and nameless fallen.

6.

An oak grove by a temple's marble columns
casts night's last shadows.
Distant, muffled, thrumming drums,
breaking waves roll in. Foes
are no longer foes. Enemies no more enemies.
Mist thin clouds,
soft and white as fine linen. Crickets. Cicadas. Sounds
from summers long past.
Birds testing new harmonies.

A girl opens two shutters to dry her hair
by the warmth of dawn. The ground
of being, the more-than-tragic found
in the everyday, in every care-
free beauty. She's eyeing a boy in a plain tunic
staring at another with myrtle eyes. Their watchful music.

Plaited like curtains, translucent as alabaster, limestone cliffs
shimmer as the wind blows
sea-ward while morning highlights last night's dying, brushed-in shadows.

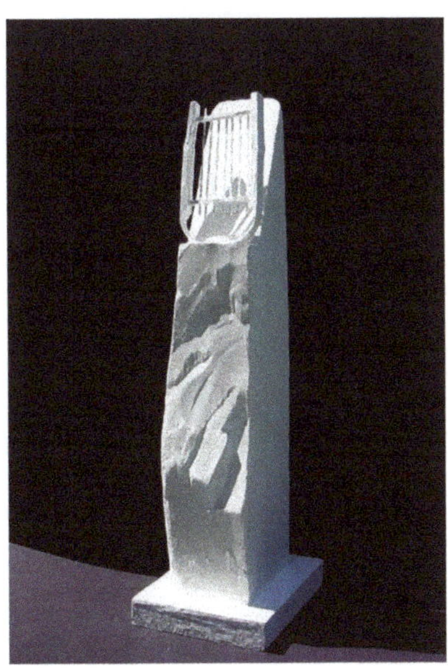

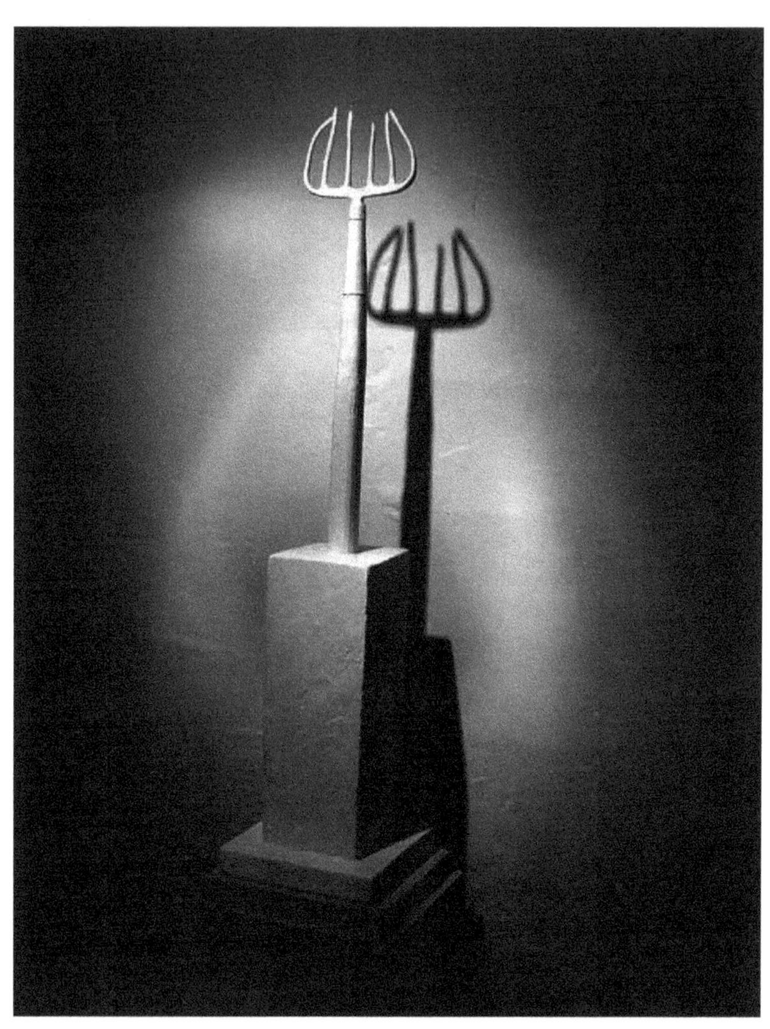

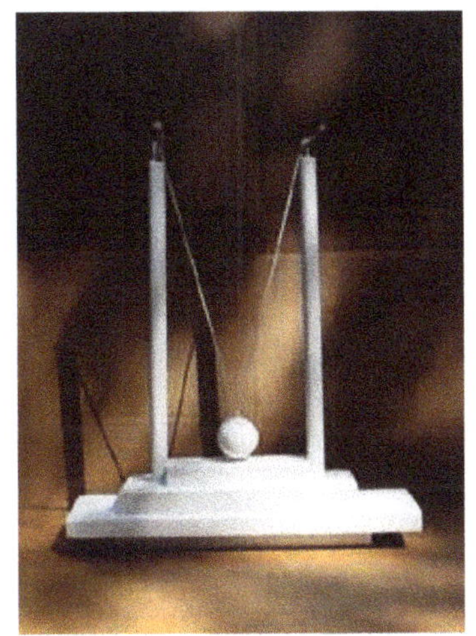

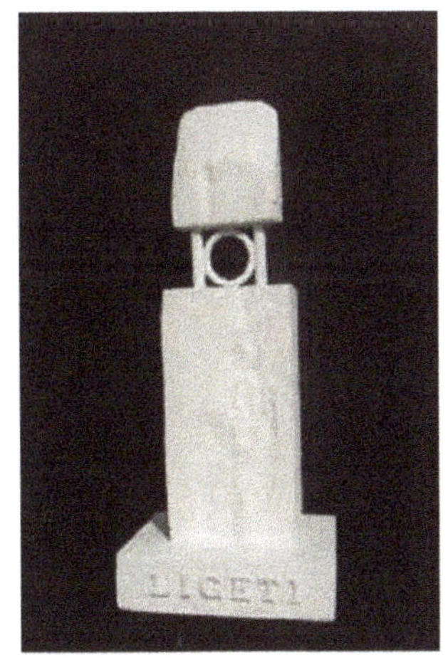
LIGETI

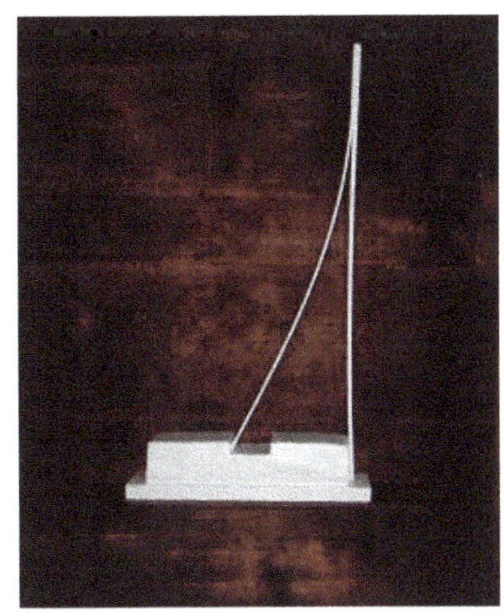

Part II

The Chosen

Near the museum, the walkways are icy-slick. Venetian
paintings hang on its walls. Jesus, saints, patrons.
Giorgione's Philosophers. Mantegna's Sebastian.
The anointing on grand display in Veronese's David
depicts a goat, a bull, and a cow guided by a ring
in its snout while it's led to the sacrifice. It's said
in Luke that Jesus, Messiah, the soon-to-be king,
must be born in the city of David. Those in the painting
observing the solemn rite appear to be wondering,
"Why was a boy, a lowly goat-herder, chosen?"
Outside, in the park, a man rends his clothes, smudges ashes
on his face, beats his chest with leafy branches, then dashes
back into the bushes. The winds turn Alaskan cold. Clouds blacken
the sun. What is the good of art when it heals no one, cures nothing?
Wars go on and on.   And the reason for choosing him is long forgotten.

Arzak, the Parthian

Lost or stolen, Arzak cannot remember which,
but gone, the only valuable thing he'd ever
owned, the ruby ring Gaius Aelius, his rich
master had given him, the gem set in silver,
its luster dazzling, one stone cut like glass
to form an oval window to peer through at
a world soaked in red, a view to surpass
all others, Gaius said on the day he chose as that
for his suicide in Brundisium, a man elected aedile
twice before he decided to enrage the emperor,
the weather fair, sea calm, sun bright while
outside his villa swifts and warblers sang for
him as he slit his wrists into a bowl his blood
stained the ruby of the ring his slave had meant to keep for good.

Now old, he squats in a grove somewhere in the Galilee.
His stools stink and steam. Figs cramp his guts.
Spirit birds fly nearer the sun. The air smells of sea
salt. His shelter is a cave the dead sleep in. Ruts
from carts mark the only road. He is as weary
as his master at his last meal, eating little. Hundreds
of people gather on a low hill, shadeless and sandy.
He moves closer, is offered fish, some fresh bread.
The basket never empties. A man speaks. "Take,
eat. Loaves, fishes. No longer hide your faces.
Strip off your soiled, worn-out garments.   For my sake,
put on the spirit's clothes I offer. Erase all traces
of your sins. Love others more than yourself," he says, looks done
until he adds, "You who out of your need for violence will leave me one by one."

And as the crowd departs, Arzak, a long freed slave,
nowhere his home, wonders if the white sliver
on his finger is a tooth from the ivory comb his master
had given him to use daily as he liked and save

if he cared to or a bit of the fish or bread he'd just eaten
or maybe a needle-thin bone he might have choked on.
He's almost naked, his loincloth in places ripped
and shredded, his arms, legs slender as the smallest

roots of the olive tree he leans against. He'd sipped
his fill of wine once upon a time. No more. Rest
is what he needs. Each night, the moon unweaves
more threads from his threadbare life. He searches

his pouch for coins. None are left. When he leaves
the world soon, he'll have given it nothing, no riches
of any sort. He'd lived a violent life. Soldier. Slave. Save me,
he begs to the place where he'd preached, now barren, now empty.

After Murillo's Flagellation of Christ

He grapples for, painfully grabs at his dirty, rumpled cloak
on the muddy floor, his hair and beard knotted, sweaty,
his body gashed by whips and nettles. Blood soaks
his loincloth, his strong back and thighs like a red rash slowly
spreading, dark and scab-like. If he could, he'd hide his nakedness,
shut his eyes like a blind man's. The ropes that lashed and beat
him dangle from a column. This is a torture chamber. Confess. Confess.
It is a tomb slashed from rock where grief is endless and hope knows only defeat.

Yet how strange, almost metaphysical, hope can be, how visionary. Their feet
like dancers', arched to float skyward despite their muscularity,
their garments thistle blue, rose rust, two angels gaze
down upon him less in human fear or horror than mystified by
what he has had to endure, to suffer, as if it does not quite faze
them, winged as they are, to see how violent humanity can be, terrified
and incomplete.

After Easter

1. Remember Me

The moon's burnt orange, far larger than a full moon,
the hazy night ballooning it after days without
rain. It's Holy Week. Even an unbeliever is not immune
to its meaning. Tonight's the seder. The drought
goes on and on. The constellations are slipping into
a massive fog bank, one by one. It's bitterly cold,
a fierce wind blowing sand across the highway,
like a desert encroaching or a waste land foretold
in myths. Perhaps none of it is real, none of it true.
Thirteen men in a room, sharing a meal. One will betray
him. Bread is his body, wine his blood. Remember me,
he beseeches. A younger man comforts him. Memory
confuses things, is often not strictly factual. Take. Eat. Drink.
Then sing praise and go to the mountain and fall away and sink into sleep.

I walk each day by the sea, gazing into its vast,
anonymous graveyard, recalling a young surfer
who drowned, pulled down by a riptide just last
week. Maybe this afternoon or some other
hour soon it will be my time to leave. At the seder,
what Jesus did was to transform mourning into
liturgy, asking his friends to eat bread, drink wine
in memory of him, he said, as if any of them later
could forget the death he'd offered them. What is true
about immortality, who knows? Suppose a sign
left behind is all it means, even if it is of an empty tomb
from which someone excitedly calls out to you, "Come
see," leaving you confused, stunned, afraid like Salome and the two
Marys after the angel of imagination told them the news and to be on their way.

2. *Pilate's Wife's Dream*

My husband's private gardens are jeweled
like fall in Gaul where in winter his men
wear the fur and hides of the beast-hordes
they put to the sword in woods thick
with trees as Nile banks with reeds.
Instead of the peace he sought the gods
have given us Jerusalem.
Rome sows confusion like Carthaginian seed
on all the earth it's salted. Tomorrow
three more to crucify. Death will wait
patiently for them, loyal as a Roman soldier
hardened by wars. Why must I dream
of the eyes of the crucified,
how like rodents' they scan the skies for signs of hawks?

3. *Good Friday Spell*

> Das ist…Karfreitagszauber, Herr! (That is…the magic of Good Friday,
> my lord!) Gurnemanz, Parsifal, Act III

He suffers on the cross still, always, the wild, kind,
baffling man who'd heal the sick, feed the hungry,
redeem sinners, end pain and suffering. The mind
is a strange place for an ancient story to be
so tenacious, compelling. All, it says, are one family.
Know it is not your fear of death alone that makes
the world holy. Dawn's glaring light this morning
is so strong, fierce, yet prolonged in its rising
as it climbs over ember-singed mountains to wake
the world up, it might be rousing itself from its own
long slumber. Celebrating a new day's beginnings,
flocks of gulls delight in gliding, dipping, soaring,

circling back and forth, then flying away, carried off by
winds, their feathers, whether white, gray, dull brown, sun-
lit and -burnished as if gleaming from within like the gold of an icon.

A storm's battering of the city has cleansed the sky. The sand
on the beach glitters, sparkles like diamond dust
or slivers and chips of amber. The northern headland
blazes. Light alone does not suffice to make the world just.
Nor does night's self-sacrifice. The tide flows in gently today,
lapping on the shore peacefully, the nearly silent, becalmed
sea a lotus-like lavender blue, the waves, as they play,
torched by sunlight, cresting into tongues of fire. Beyond
the realm of history, somewhere in the life and death of his story,
an innocent man is being crucified. Look, here, how even ravens,
black and somber as priests, cawing, mourn on dunes, along the seawall.
Yet the sun, the honey-colored sun, pours out its bounty over sea
and land, its light like a rite, like the grail shining in its shrine in Parsifal.
Christ of the dunes, of burgeoning spring, of late March, compassion's
measure, as you suffer on your cross, why confuse us with your death day's beauty?

4. *Stabat Mater (after Szymanowski)*

The wind, sighing, retreats from the stinging stench of death
in the air. The sun, grieving, hides from its burden of sight.
In this place, it's hard to speak, to cry, to take a breath
that is not painful. The sky is dark, yet cruelly bright.
The young for the old, a poet wrote, that is tragedy.
Jesus. Persephone. Lear howling over his daughter,
Cordelia. But isn't it obscene to flee from death into story,
myth? A mother weeps, wonders why, receives no answer.
Another embraces her son against her breast, a boy killed
by a bomb that set their village on fire. Another waits
by her dying daughter's bedside. What evil has willed
it so? Yet another hesitates outside a door. Who hates

her son enough to execute him for no reason? And who is that there,
see?, from sorrow and loss rending her flesh, tearing her hair?
Wherever a child is suffering, in a city, town, on farmland, at sea,
or on a bone-bearing barren hill, a mother stands grieving. Call her Mary.

5. *Centurion*

The Gauls across the river keep yelling
curses, re-grouping in the woods.
I didn't mean to leave you,
Lucius. They tell me the war is over.
But I can hear their shouting.

Our company has drawn the sun's attention.
Yesterday, it killed Demetrius.
Death is our gift to the fatality
of time. I love the sun and stars
more than most.

I never rest but watch the river, farms,
and mountains. I know every secret
of month and year.
You are goodness. Life is
horror.

I can't drink wine because of the danger.
I miss the easiness of bed
and slumber. On the third day
of Quintillis, I sent you
a tender sign

of summer, a shadow from a tree near
our encampment. Do not hide
your face. Do not turn
away in anger. I have news
that will make

all Rome rejoice. Our days are hard.
the gods' nights endure
forever, yet I have seen the face
of one I crucified who died
enraptured.

6. *The Deposition*

In Caravaggio's painting, it is easy to see why
the bleak, dark background in the picture
was left blank, empty, endlessly deep as if to try
to depict oblivion were hopeless. Mary weeps, the beloved
disciple is doubled over, his cloak blazing red,
redder than blood, redder than the tunic of Nicodemus
who looks stunned, glaring at any viewer too impure
to witness the scene, appearing to dare us
not to stay silent while two more women lament over
the body being laid out on a slab of brown-black stone,
thick and inhumanly heavy. Where does the light that shines
on this fraught entombment come from? An unseen, alien sun that, alone,
burns beyond the visible, penetrating the obscurity that surrounds it by
illuminating the aftermath of death it means to show us, the terror of it and its pity?

7. *Vigil*

Eleven desolate men wait in a hot,
windowless, upper room more
barren than a tomb staring not
at each other but a barred door
and bare walls, feeling alone,
abandoned, betrayed by their fear
of dying like him, heavy and stone-
like in their silence, nothing clear
anymore, only these mournful,
disquieted men, trying to remember
what he'd told them, his sayings,
stories and parables accounting
for all he'd left them, all they can know
about why he suffered and died,
two thousand and counting years ago.

8. **The Appearance**

Unable to sleep, an old man lies restless on his bed,
staring at another like him stretched out across
from him on a mattress flat as a slab in a morgue.
Soon a nurse or doctor will barge in to see
who in the ward's failed to weather the night.
Not him who's borne worse storms than most.
Fluid in his lungs almost drowned him once,
tugging him back to Texas. But his bleary eyes
cleared. He survived. And now the naked phantom
man with the face white as linen sits again at the foot
of his bed, his voice like a flute's or oboe's sweetly
rueful as he says, What's more to fear? Here, he says, pointing,
or there, each time smiling brighter than before. Nothing
more than a deathbed vision, the old man supposes. But whose?

9. *The Inn at Emmaus*

Who is the third who walks always beside you?
   T.S. Eliot, The Waste Land, l. 360

Winds tear and scatter petals from a garden
behind the wayside inn, a storm
hiding in the desert eager to unburden
itself of rage, to form
new clouds, thin and white, drifting
peacefully through the sky, the world no longer maddened
by lightning, nor by its heaving
thunder onto an anxious humanity saddened
by fear. Look. There's a strange man in the inn
offering his unhealed
wounds for you to touch, to feel his pain begin
again in you. What has he revealed
to you of a reality that is not sorrow
alone, nor suffering, nor spring yet either, whatever might come tomorrow?

10. *Easter in Kure Beach, on Clingmans Dome*

a.

Suppose this place in April is an intimation of paradise. Waves break over rocks
and tug shell shards back into natural sluices. The washed sand where logger-
head turtles lay their eggs gleams like sugar. Laurel oak and live oak, loblolly
pine, hornbeam, ironwood, flowering dogwood, and red cedar forest the higher
ridges, and in the wetland swales between the dunes grow cypress, red maple, red
bay, cattails and marsh grasses. Deer, wild goat, mink hide in dappled shadows.
Each spring, first come the warblers, the hawks and other raptors follow. In the
harbor, trawlers launch for shrimp and crabs while other boats sail for distant
lands. In the morning, friends gather on a slip of an islet to watch the sun rise; in
the evening, to see it set. Tourists hover, all times of day, in small hotel lobbies,
waiting for surreys to take them to the sites cited in their guidebooks. What will

they remember of their visits there, take home with them to ponder, tell stores,
however far-fetched, of what they might have seen, otherwise hidden from their
eyes, by Kure Beach's teeming enveloping Easter Day clarity?

b.

Hike again through tickets of underbrush,
foxtail fern, lupine, wood anemone
to a ravine's piles of lumber and scree,
eons-old boulders. Rest. Don't rush.
Cool off under the shade of hickory,
yellow birch, fir needles. Cross the brook
nimbly, its thick slabs slick with algae.
You'll be there soon. Pause. Look
up. You're close to the summit, your journey
over, inspired by the view it gave you
when young. Late in life, what will you say
of it, as if it were new? The way ahead is steep,
harder to climb now. To believe only in what is true
matters most to you, doesn't it? There's always time enough for sleep.

Here is a wilderness where you hid when you could from time,
from family and friends, retreating from bad news,
fearful stories, disasters. Believe me. I'm
not saying death didn't obsess you already. You left clues

from your past for me to know better, the near total dark
of the forest where you would struggle with vines,
ivy, briars, and brush. The oak and hickory bark
was black as duff or the fungus growing from stumps, signs,

you decided, of mammoth trees that once rose there, the wet air
always drizzling. So began your quest for God, the canopy diffusing only a bare
half-light, like poetry or mythology you insisted later, as if the woods were inviting
you in to its vision of holiness, the reality hidden within it revealed by the hazy
light of spring.

After Mantegna

His flesh is white as a tree branch stripped
of bark. Muscles, taut as hide scraped,
washed clean of blood, stretched in the sun
to dry. Eyes, transalpine blue, bright
with a vision of paradise. Nothing
about this painting ought to be true. Not
the distant city, the column he's strapped
to, the ruins of the temple he's poised on.
There is no one else in the picture. No
centurion, no soldier. The arrows have pierced
his body, their shafts penetrating deep
into his flesh in a work of art, hanging in a museum
where wounds like his bleed in room after
room as if pleading for freedom from pain and peace forever.

I remember a friend's photograph of his father
in his uniform before he left for D-day
and the beach on which he died before
his son was born. It was like an icon
of a saint, of martyrdom to him. When he
looked at it, he'd try to imagine
his father's fear and suffering and pain
and not flinch from the horror of it, as if
his father's boyish face and smiling eyes
in the picture evoked hopes for a life he was
never to live, save, in a way, in the images
of soldiers' bodies lying on Omaha my friend
examines daily, wondering which one is his old man's,
who, while he's dying too fast to pray, might wish to live forever.

Priest

for Father Geoffrey Glaser

1.

The moon is burnt orange, a harvest moon
in early spring. Tonight's the seder.
In four days, the crucifixion.
Rain, intemperate weather
for this time of year with a cold
wind that blows
in from the north. Every death is foretold
somehow though no one knows
why. The storm-wet, smoldering moon
will set soon,
and the time will come when my life is undone
forever. That hour obsesses
me, my emptiness, my spiritual darkness
before the perpetually too-late-rising of the savior sun.

2.

He hangs on his cross still, the wild kind
man who cured the sick, fed the hungry,
forgave sinners. The spirit is a blind
man, a beggar, without family.
We were made from dust
for mercy's sake. Take,
eat, drink. Trust
in eternity to rectify history's
terrors, its tragedies.
If it is death that makes
the world holy, then it is holy.

Look, Lord. I wait outside the empty
tomb of your days and pray to say, Come see,
confused and stunned as Mary.

3.
Jesus of the desert, of a reluctant spring,
of red-tailed hawks, flycatchers, cactus
wrens, white-winged doves soaring,
dipping, flying away, return to us.
The sun is a jewel-like amber
with a glare like that off burnished steel,
hotter than summer's,
the clouds like gold-adorned fingers
as it pours its light
upon us who feel
in need of your rites,
parched as we are and thirsty for libation.
And your sky, the heavenly sky, is a lotus-
like lavender blue too beautiful not to get drunk on.

4.
What might it mean to ask
of your friends when you die,
who survive you,
to give them the task,
or maybe we should try
to think of it as a favor true
to your wishes, to transform grieving
for you into liturgy
as Jesus at the seder did requesting

they break bread, drink wine in memory
of me,
he said, however mythologically
we understand him, as if his followers could forget the cost
of the death he gave them, the lives they'd lost.

5.
Messiaen's music. We are all immigrants, exiled,
wandering, sun-struck, reviled,
famished, nearly dead
from hunger, fatigue. Imagine a sea's
coastline. Follow its birds come
to your new home
in sympathy with the histories
you've fled
from. There, in your fantasy where it's early dawn, pelicans, geese,
ravens, plovers, gulls rest on the beach at peace
until the sun, in a joyous sight,
breaks through clouds when they suddenly all take flight,
all the flocks of them freely flapping as one to delight you, cacophonously
chirruping, chattering, cawing, calling. Listen. This is compassion.
This is light's mystery.

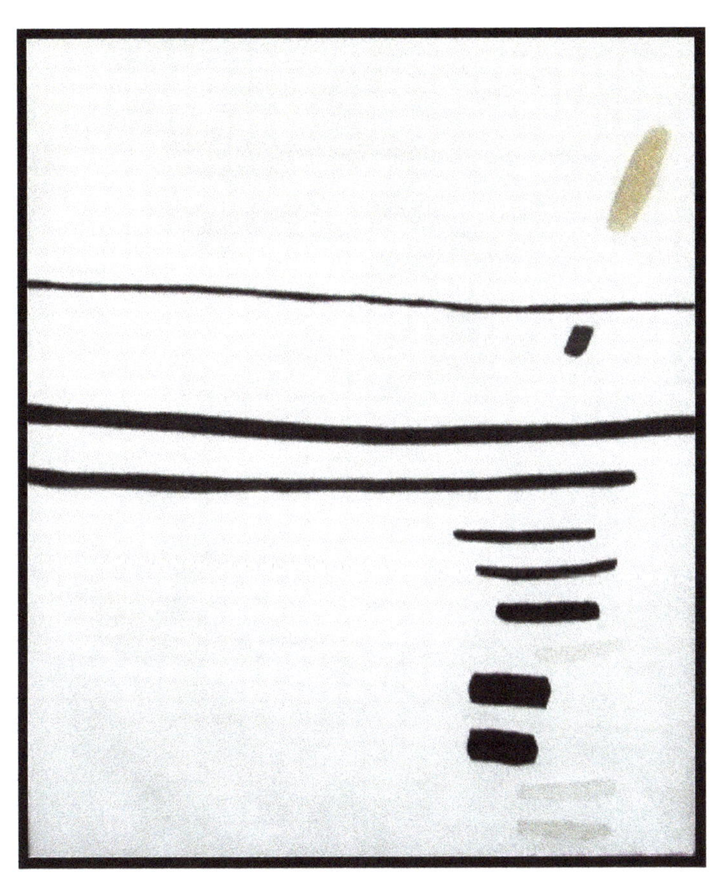

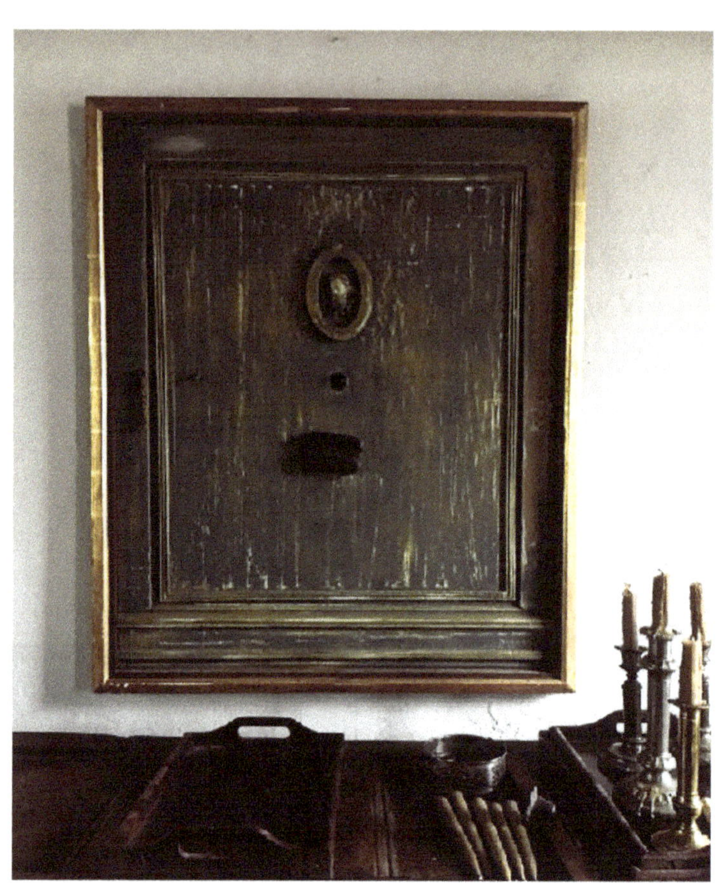

Part III

Consciousness

1.

Rocks chipped flat, smoothed by rain
to pebbles, ground by waves to sand
command the beach where they remain
for a day or two along the strand
before being washed back to sea.
Years ago, I found a wooden fragment
of a small statue, a torso, in the debris
left by a storm like something sent
there for me to find as I strolled the beach.
One leg, one arm was missing, the rest
of its body mostly eroded. Only its face
stayed expressive as if capable of speech
or song, darkened like driftwood. What place
do we take in the cosmos when possessed
by something, somehow, to drown in its immensity?

2.

A crab on its back kicks its legs.
Gulls, ravens peck at it, hungry
for meat as it aches for the tide
to carry it back out of the dregs
of bits of driftwood, pieces of sea-
weed. But it has nowhere to hide
from the man with a stick poking
it to see if it is truly alive or only
dying so slowly he cannot know
which it is. It's as if the man's taunting
it to prod it toward where it wants to be

as the waves fall back into the storm-
blackened sea that intends no harm
as it litters the beach with piles of detritus.
Consciousness in its cruelty, its sublime carelessness.

3.

Plovers skittering the shoreline, gulls' cries,
waves
chipping the cliff face.
A pelican
hovers, waits for its flock, then flies
toward the headland in an arc its wings trace
on its way
toward vanishing.
A man
watches as if he were imagining a different place.

The crescent moon dips as it sets, Yesterday,
unsurprisingly,
this was how consciousness
began:
leeward breezes dying as crows beautifully stay
in the air just by gliding while a crab boat on the horizon
of all
the visible world
traverses the span
of it by sailing toward harbor and the rising light of the sun.

Shame

1.

What is seen shadowed in a cave by flames might be more true
than a sunlit world. The night you told me you were leaving for Paris
the next day, the full moon, shining through my bedroom window,
cast your shadow on the blank wall behind where you, still naked, stood.

That image is still fixed in my mind. You had seen what I had seen, knew
what I knew: beyond the desolation of clear cutting, the callous
desecration, abandonment of the land, the waste of years, how,
in a rain forest, a fallen redwood will often rot to some natural good,

sustaining lives of things far less monumental, imposing than its had been:
the mysterious thriving of a forest floor, the paradisal greens of vine,
fern, and moss as well as the tangled thicket we had yet to hike through,
the arched bridge over the rampaging waterfall we had to cross before we
reached

the glacier, the scary ledges we risked to get there and back. Is yours or mine
the harder trail to explore now? I'm trying to find your shadow, I've searched
many nights for you in my dreams, wanting to tell you, no, finally to confess
to you how I'd failed you those days you lay in bed ravaged by disease, sleep-
less, hopeless.

2.
I might want to be a child again, roaming in a forest,
hoping to get lost, to forget, to vanish into the dark
of hickory, pine, sycamore, to hide beneath leaves'
and needles' canopies, obscuring the sun. The best

time for regrets is night, only the summer's fireflies
visible, flitting and blinking erratically, like sparks
embers spit skyward when angered. What grieves
a boy lying in bed after a long day spent wandering

in woods, wading in a creek, drinking its pure cold,
water, lying down on a bank strewn with weeds,
reeds, moss, creating a necklace of flowers, bold
in their bright costume colors, wearing it like beads

around his neck? I am a man grown old, not alone
but solitary. I live by the ocean. Yet I still dream
at night of woods and hiking and a simple stone
I found by a stream and pocketed as if its soullessness could save me.

3.

A summer sweet Southern night. Fireflies returning. A quiet
sky. Cattle roaming through grassy pastures. We sit
face to face behind a barn's door. His fingers gently
explore the budding whiskers on my cheeks. I let

his hands stay there. Lips closed, we kiss. That's it.
That's all. The rest I fantasize and save for later.
Two boys' too quick consummation. Me after,
afraid of confessing my secret, the news not fit

for others to hear, ashamed as I am of who I must be.
Play make-believe. The better part of life
is imaginary. He and I in bed where no one can see
us, embracing, making love. It's more real than a movie

is when I stare up at the screen. No tension, no strife,
no struggle, no fear. His hands touch me, caress
my body as we lie side by side.   I possess
his secret now, he mine. And it is wonderful, that serenity.

4.

Words confuse the things you meant to mean.
Nothing written ever gets it right.
But to be no more
yourself forever feels shameful. Hungry and lean,

a coyote wanders the dunes, sea gulls, pelicans, weak
from their long journey,
linger on the shore.
It is a foggy morning, too cold for you to seek

the hope you're searching for. Have you forgotten
what frightens
you most? Meek,
you would be, and innocent. Attend to presentiments,

then: a crow foraging for carnage in a trash can,
the sea washing away debris as the sun warms the sand,
a log, black as a priest's cassock, rolling in with the rising tide.
and a man (maybe suicidal) wading in up to his thighs, waiting

and waiting,

unable to decide.

5.

I wake to a light colder than anything
I'd felt in the dark. It is early fall,
the coast fogged in and all
the streets drenched as after storms in spring.

The full moon is frozen, chilly white. I
watched it through the long night
shining through my window, its icy light
cracking at dawn with an inhumanly icy

cry. Water. Light. The tide's receding.
Why do I feel unready, naked?
Humiliation is this morning's sun offering
its gifts of clarity to me, warming my bed.

If it is not reality we long for, what is this
sorrow about? Not mine only,
but the world's? Maybe it's not bliss,
exactly, too bitter for that, but why deny its beauty?

6

The evening is restless as mist. The starless city
is lit by streetlights, by San Francisco's
nightly glow, its dread of dark, its petty
infidelities, the stories it repeats down rows

upon rows of houses. The Presidio's massive, high
cliffs are too steep for anyone to climb,
though nobly tall, faraway. It's a long time
since people have told the truth about being happy.

I try to be stoic, though I'm ashamed of how old age
has changed me. Why must I choose, this late,
between a world on fire and a wild, darkening sea?
What doubts I have are not mine only. Rage

and hate translate us all. I stroll seaside, studying
things as they drift at tide's edge, shells broken
by waves, a floating blue bottle, an amassing,
tangled mess of amber-green seaweed, a rotten

clump of leafy driftwood. In the half-light, they look
almost beautiful, composed,. The wide strand
sparkles white as snow. I remember best how you took
my breath away when we were young, then, unashamed, clasped my hand.

Waiting for Grace

1.

Through the village, by the wide river's strict edges,
people wander. The era of The Three Great Griefs
shows no signs of ending, darkens the eyes of sages
with shadows of regret. Why does every leaf
in autumn fall into the heart? Young, they moved
through life too quickly. Old, they see themselves
betrayed by time, by dreams that played what's proved
to be a too seductive music. They drink from wells
of memory to quench their thirsts, to wet their parched
throats so that they might sing, with drums and bells,
their ancient chants. A wren passes over their temple
garden. A martin's sapphire plumage dazzles at a window.
The world is as it is in the empire of signs, observed, watched,
cared for. Everything is free and joyous, everything is simple.
Attend to what is there, meaningless and clear. Think nothing of tomorrow.

2.

Yet, as if intent on something more real,
all day I stare through a window.
What sorrow is it that I feel
when I think of tomorrow,
white clouds fading into a darkening
sky, a storm looming over the horizon?
My white, shaggy hair is dangling
over my shoulders, my face is unshaven.
My love's dark brown eyes
smile in wonder at life's mysteries
as he gnaws a honey crisp apple

fresh from the bowl. So simple,
isn't it, sometimes, the reason
we give for living? As if each moment could be
a kind of waiting for grace despite the horrors of history.

3.

The past. The pressure of the unspeakable
that longs to be spoken. The mind
is a mirror. Polish it. See
how dust clings to it, how blind
you are to mistake the face
shown in it for your own. The tree
of memory has many
tangled roots and branches. The door
of its house no handle to open
it with, its windows no latch to free
you from it, unlock it with. What are imagination,
language, artistry, creation for
if not to mirror back to you who you are?
If the only glass you need to reflect you is transparency,
polish it. Wipe it clean of steam from your breath.

4.

In deep shadows, plovers, sandpipers turn into carved
birds, stone or driftwood statues set on dunes.
The world is adrift, at sea, starved
for meaning. Unobserved,
you study the houses around you, lit by moon's
descent, where neighbors lie sleeping. A mist
is gathering strength before first light.

You want to say, All is good, All is right,
but cannot say it, the world like runes
you cannot translate. Yet time appears suspended,
if only for an instant, while a hazy dawn, almost invisibly,
slowly breaks over the eastern hills. Whatever life you've missed
cannot matter now, nor your dreams of awakening elsewhere.
The world is your home and you must leave it, with every care
you bear for it weighing upon your heart even as you wait like a lover to be kissed.

Bliss

1.

It is said the storied masters of gardens
dance wherever flowers bloom. Imagine,
then, how men, women, joined by friends
might laugh into winkled old age, as children
laugh, though now white-haired, frail, and thin.
But as they sing and dance, like people drunk
on joy, they grieve, too, having learned, just in
time, how beauty makes fear inescapable. Think
of a river, clear and tranquil, as the bearer of
the silence of ultimate things as it flows, beloved
and mysterious, toward the sea. Dying, do we sink
deep into its bed of forgetfulness? A monk
might claim that oblivion is but another word for bliss,
that everything is finally one: as it was, as it will be, so it is.

2.

Why must I choose between an earth I love
and a darkening sea? What doubts I have
are not mine only. Around, below, above
me is everything I need, just this world, to save
me from myself. What remains? My life
is fading like a tide on its way out leaving
behind on the beach fragments of things rife
with memories, glossy wet, brightly shining
under a cloudless sky and a blinding sun.
Let them be. Soon, a rising sea will return
to claim them, to take them back into its
restless, nameless enormity. Sublimity, let's
face it, is unbearable. I've lived my days as if I
believed only in particulars. Why betray them now?

3.

Jasmine. Magnolia. Roses. Their perfumes belong here
with me in my room as I listen, sleepless, to the ocean's
roaring not far from my home. It is a sound to fear,
some neighbors say. I know what they mean. Switch scenes.
House lights flickering off a lake's calm waters. Mallards
sleepily drifting. A waxing moon under white sheets of clouds.
A dam overflowing into a creek. Winds rustling through yards
hidden by long-leaf pine, hickory, oak. Late night enshrouds
daytime's life in dreams, revives memories. The hot, humid air.
A car door slammed. Footsteps on pavement, on crunchy dry sand.
Two boys meeting in secret because it is necessary. All they dare
do risking their futures, hopes for a better life somewhere. Understand
what I mean by writing this. Paradise is the joy of any past happiness
brought back to life. His body like flowers blossoming over me in our moment of bliss.

The Moral Imperative of Intelligence

Louder and louder, eternal waves break on the shore
where Demosthenes orates to himself over the roar
of the sea during a winter storm. Nothing is more
dangerous than a country and its people's self-deceit
and ignorance. A lone, glossy black swan gleams
in the foam as, with the daring and pride of a fleet
of triremes on their way to war, it flies toward
its death. Could it be peace, reunion it dreams
of as it leaves the world? Men of the bow, the sword
seek fame. But who praises intelligence, builds
monuments to its rarity? Athens, defeated, is in danger.
Is it knowledge, the light flashing off the swan's feathers
as the sun breaks through the clouds? He's so thrilled
by its grievous beauty he falls silent. And three centuries later,
in his villa, Cicero, aware his life's over, the imminent loss
of the Republic soon to be completed, preparing to slit his wrists,
gazes up at the sky, knowing when wisdom lies in contemplating the cosmos.

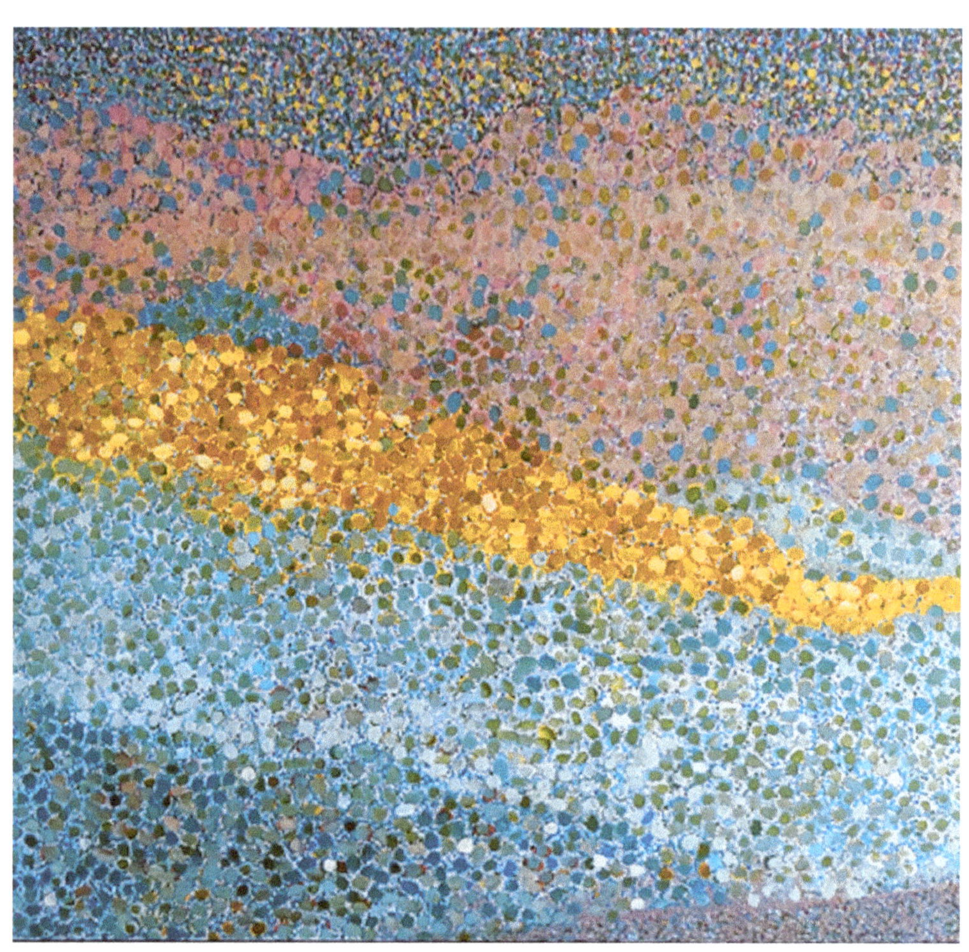

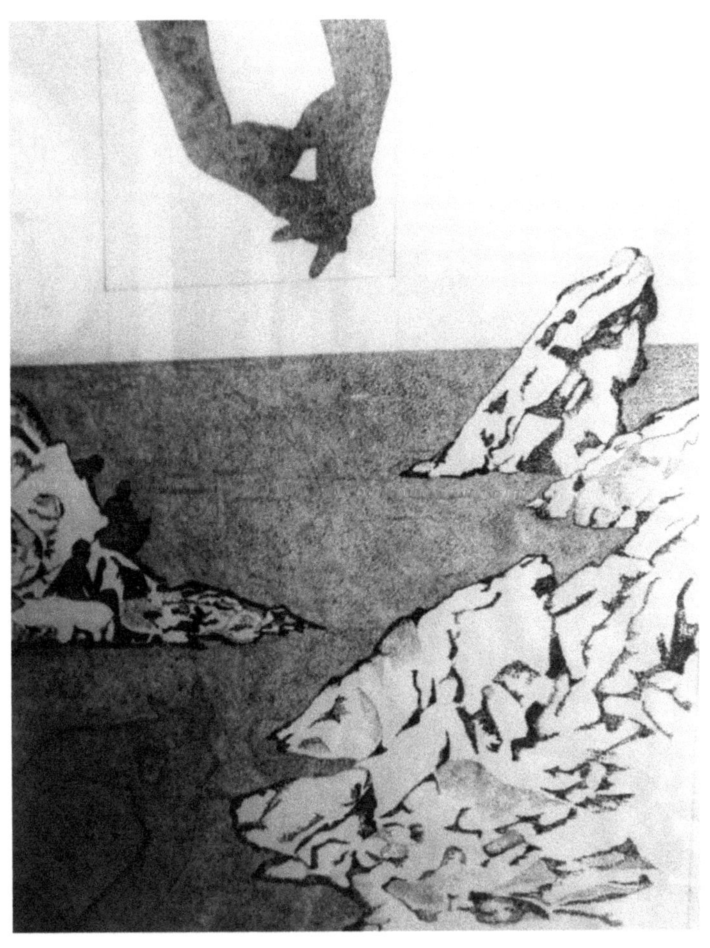

Part IV

A Death in Laguna Beach

1.

We stand on a sheer cliff overlooking the beach. It's high tide.
A schooner skims the horizon. Though it'll clear soon, the sky's
still covered by clouds the mottled gray of wet newspaper.
Jay is groggy, half asleep, wearing only a t-shirt and faded Levi's.

He doesn't believe in god or any afterlife and had to rouse
himself back to life this morning, brooding about suicide
until he recalled his plans to go with Norm to Baja by summer.
What scares me most is how much dying feels like an empty house,

he says, abandoned, dark, unfit to live in, unvisited, remote, lonely.
I've never been this alone before, though it's hard to know why.
Invisibility is no surprise.
                              I love how this patch of scrub brush
kneels toward the hills after suffering for years from winds off the sea.

Sometimes I feel like that, beaten down by years of feeling this crush
or that, yet always having to keep it a secret, imagining a reality
I could survive in no matter how cheap or false or phony
my disguises were. I can't pretend anymore. I'm afraid to die.

2.

No, he did not attend a fancy boarding school in Switzerland.
That print hanging on his wall is not a real Modigliani.
He can't speak fluent French. Never studied in Montpelier.
He never danced at a party with Isherwood, hand in hand.

His father wasn't a wealthy ad man. There is no rich family.
He never slept with Tony Perkins. And so on. He's lots to say
on the matter of truth telling if he could find the bravery
to confess, to face his shame and embarrassment. Probably not,

he admits, with so little time left to excuse the past as each cough
spasm, new pain or old reminds him.

He stares east. A hot
day is on its way, he can tell, as the sun drags itself over
the mountains. The beach will be free of fog and mist no later than noon.

Todd, biker, dark and handsome. Nelly, funny, witty Jeff. Alec, surfer
blond and sinewy. He's slept with them all, many more, had a lover
or two. All that's true, real he insists.

He's still young, eager, good-looking.
But who will want him after his his arm is sawed off? Why struggle to go on living?

3.

Dante's packed, body pressed against
body, the ocean from the deck,
glittering like jewels or precious
metals, the horizon molten

into gold, the sea platinum
smooth, the silver waves
scattering opalescent pebbles
and shells on the beach.

The day's intensified by the promise
of sex. It's Fourth of July.
The crowd on the dance
floor roars louder than the Pacific

as fires are lit for the barbecue. When night
comes, the high-flying rockets, the beauty
of the fireworks reignite our dreams of a Peter
Pan world claimed as only ours by all us lost boys.

4.

For a few weeks, mid-summer,
before he was ill, Jay and I lived
in his apartment on Oak Street, its
garden rich with fuchsias, bougainvillea,

hydrangeas. We'd watch
sunset's russet dust
settle on the roofs below
and wonder aloud about how

much time we had left together
to remember each other
by. He started to cry,
why?, his cheeks red with a hectic

flush against his black wavy
hair. Did I ever really know
him, my cipher friend, lying,
when he did, from dread of being no one?

5.

We sit side by side in the bar, staring at
Route 1 traffic. Last call. Rat-a-tat-tat.
Jay plays a one-armed riff with a teaspoon
on a table. Norm feeds the jukebox.

Morrison wails Weill again. O moon
of Alabama. Cool, he says. Jim rocks.
Jay's drink is a pale, waxy green and tastes,
he says, like waxy honey. He makes

a face and smiles. It is time to leave, go home.
The short uphill walk back takes
longer since he must pause to breathe.
I sleep in the guest bedroom, Norm and Jay

in his beside it. I cannot keep myself, a little drunk,
from hearing their moans and sighs. Norm's not going away,
He will stay to the end and, for years after, grieve.
But for now, making love, they're making it last one more day.

6.

For six months or more, he'd thought the knot
in his wrist was a quirk of his zeal at the gym,
buffed to look like the bodies he lusted for,
humpy as a wrestler, yet slim, lithe as a track star.

He tells me the news about his cancer
like a witness to an accident, dazed by
the carnage, the road ahead impassable.
Two years later, an hour or so after we had talked

on the phone, his voice hoarse and frightened,
an artery ruptured in his lungs. The blood
pooled around the chair where he'd sat.
While we were talking, he'd also been listening to

the Willow Song from Rossini's tragic-comic Otello,
von Stade singing, sad, plaintively sweet: Oh,
willow of love's joy, merciful shadow of sorrow,
let the breezes sing through you gently while they lament me.

7.

The night's been made for making out. Faces glow from coals
in the barbecue on the deck. The roses are livid pinks
and reds in the blue-tinted spotlights. Dying stinks,
Jay says. Brendon vows to quit enacting his tearoom roles
for us. Some kid is crying in the kitchen, trying hard to
stop. A whoop of laughter from the living room. A tango.
A kick line. There's jazzing in the garden. Jay's too sick
not to feel out of place, a bit unreal, half-alive. He asks Colin
to change the record from show tunes to Mozart, his Third Violin
Concerto. Colin ponders. Did Mozart ever compose any bad music?
With two fingers of his remaining hand, Jays gently studies, traces
a few new wrinkles around my unmasked eyes. Of course, it's no sin.
he says, but in a way you're beginning to say goodbye, too. All these lovely faces.
He surveys the room and yard. All in disguises, all in costumes, each
grinning like a pumpkin.

8.

Two years after Jay died, early in the epidemic, the plague began ravaging Laguna
Beach. By the mid nineteen nineties, of our group of friends, there were only four
or five of us left alive. Thirty or more had died. Those that survived moved or stayed
away for good.

Forty years after, gay Laguna Beach, the Provincetown of the West some wrongly
called it, has vanished. Now it belongs mostly to moguls, successful techies, high
priced lawyers, or movie people, heterosexual, rich, and right wingers.

I write this last paragraph and suddenly it is a summer morning in the middle seven-
ties on Oak Street again. Scattered in patches, random, free as weeds in the garden,
golden poppies glow iridescently. Fuchsias and camellias bloom. Bougainvillea

dangles from rooftops, fences, trellises. Scotch broom, daisies, calla lilies, scarlet salvia, hollyhocks, nasturtiums flourish haphazardly all over the yard, sneaking into the shallow gulley that parallels the narrow road. A sprinkler sprays the lawn, opening and closing like a fan. Stripped to his briefs, Jay is painting a lamp with black lacquer.

A scrub jay caws in an orange tree. A lizard scurries across the patio. Two warblers sing wheezily. Jay lies down on a blanket, face up, eyes open, and mops his forehead with a towel. At the horizon, clearly visible from where we stand on the hill, a flat white sky is mirrored by the Pacific's glassy blue.

Jay pinches his biceps. South of town, night's few remaining lights are vanishing into day while the two points of the northern bay's crescent flash like a scimitar.

He starts to recite Chaucer to me in middle English, a long passage from The Knight's Tale. Why he loves that tale the most I've never known. He's eloquent and moving, not bragging about how much he remembers and perfectly recites each line slowly, greedily, savoring it.

The beauty of its poetry dazzles him and me. When he's finished, he laughs and takes a cigarette from the pack lying beside him, lights it, exhales. He's a perfectly lovely man, happy on a joyous day. And he makes me happy too. We're friends to the end. It's a year before he'll hear the bad news. A tail-less lizard darts from a rock and slithers between us deeper into the grass. Jay stands up to smoke, his arms and chest spattered with paint.

Later that day, as we wait on a cliff overlooking a narrow beach for sunset to begin, he asks me again if I have ever noticed how all the sparse scrub bushes along its edges bend eastward as if praying together, kneeling as one toward morning and sunrise as if forced to prostrate themselves by the sea's winds every night?

No, I say, not lying, I never have. And look around at all the low lying, sturdy, spindly brush, as if for the first time. They do look a bit like petitioners, seeking relief. Or mendicants. Or willing worshippers at the prayer rail.

We gaze west, waiting until the last filament of light between sea and sky burns out, then turn back and walk side by side, in silence, to The Breakers where we'll join our friends.

Forty Years After

Wild sea winds rattle the skylight.
Waves crash, echo in caves.
A pale moon seeps through restless shades.

Do not try to resist or fight
it. Who knows what saves
you, even a dream that fades

away by day, that makes right
your mistakes? A vase
full of flowers. Sunlit glades

in woods. The sudden sight
of him on a staircase or in doorways.
How he once more wades

into the sea, holds you tight
in the morning. A grave's
a mighty place to dream of, decades

after he died, the plague's blight
upon him as a nurse shaves
him. Everyone trades

places with the past at night
when we all are slaves
to our desires, to whatever persuades

us they're true. The winds quiet. The light
goes silent. What is he who craves
you still, however much he evades

your touch? His body is white
as a ghost's. Another ghost laves
and soothes his lesions. We are renegades

from life, we survivors, who shamelessly write
lies about why we never forgave
ourselves for staying. What god invades

you as you sleep, that never speaks of right
or wrong? What priest prayed
with you over his body, promising you better days?

A bird in an after flight
of desire, for a moment waylaid
in your life, flies in one window, out another, back into the night

while wild sea winds rattle the skylight,
waves crash, echo in caves,
and a pale moon dances like restless spirits prancing on graves.

A Summer Night

There's a rubbery mole on his shoulder. His hand,
fumbling, reaches higher as the bed board creaks.
A diver's thighs. A sunbather's sweat. The sand
paper grain of his calluses, the bristles in his cheeks,
balls persimmon sour, his calves tasting of sea salt.
Tar-shiny hair and pubes, thin coal-black eyebrows,
irises simmering blue. We knew it was no one's fault
it could last only a few hours. No tomorrows. No vows.
One body slips inside another slowly as snakes
might hesitate before sloughing off their former skin.
Stiff pricks, aroused nipples, hard and purple brown.
What need, what desire, what frenzy is it that makes
flesh try to explode like galaxies or, like nebulae, to spin
until, like the universe some day, it inevitably cools down?

A man beautiful as the ocean off Laguna in summer
while a schooner skims the horizon and the sky's
flecked with sapphire on a morning gray as wet paper.
I watch him dress into his briefs, t-shirt, tight levies
and wonder why I don't believe in God, religious
as I am in the ways of love. Parents should be kinder
to their children, they to them, I guess. How gorgeous
he looks by full daylight. And a good friend can matter
a lot. On the front yard's cliff, small rocks dislodge easily
and frequently fall into the sea. Some days are hard
to live past dawn, to go on. What does it mean not to be?
Hope is the same as quiet. He stands at the edge of the yard,
turns, and waves, then saunters cockily over to the zig-zag, wooden
staircase down to the beach like one who is terrified by how quickly he'll
be forgotten.

After Seeing Of an Age

A night like any other in late summer. The Breakers'
deck packed long after the bar had closed, no
more dancing, no music. The windows' shutters
locked till morning. Men checking whom to go
home with almost too late, so quiet you could hear
waves lapping the piers a hundred feet away.
He tapped my shoulder, sipped the last of his beer,
said Hi, and that was that. How long did we stay
together, talking, laughing, confessing, making love? Less
than twenty four hours, more than a lifetime. Joy
is often the same as sorrow. I gave him my address.
He gave me his. We wrote a few times. Years later,
I saw him in a bar in another city. We slowly walked together
to my place, hugged, and ended it. The love of my life. That beautiful boy.

When We Were One Tide

1.

His knotted straw hair was always gritty with sand,
his bathing suit of cut-off jeans constantly wet,
his eyes most sparkling when gazing seaward, one hand
on my shoulder. His favorite time of day was early sunset.

At dusk once, he knifed his name in rock face, cut
deep into the schist. He loved men's bodies, fed
on their beauty, refused ever to grow old, though in his gut
he knew he must no matter what he thought or said

to me one night in bed. "Wait for high tide, the stars
to shine. Then you must really let me go.
I promise I won't return to haunt you. It's like in wars
People die. Are listed as missing. But you know."

The plague soon followed. I've hunted the deserted coast
for him, our friends each day since. Maybe it was wrong
of him to write me the night he vanished, "Whatever it cost,
I've loved my life and all my guys. But it's time to go. So long."

2.

The arc of the sky, barely visible through the fog, is
his breath, the wind his pulse, the day as it clears
his sea-blue eyes. What I need most now is this,
this perpetual cresting of waves near me, what fears

I know not mine alone as waves break hard on the beach,
recede into the Pacific. This is my life's sole solace.
Rapture, if it exists at all, if we can reach
out to touch it, must lie waiting in the repetitive pace

of tides, in the seeming stillness of the sea between
one wave and another, in the quiet of the exhausted
water, dying, lapping on the sand, as in the dream
lovers sometimes have that their love is never dead

since beginnings and ends are the same, the tide
rushing in or retreating. I stand in the ocean, a few
yards away from the rocky face on the sea's side
of the promontory where he carved his name, where you still ride

the waves as they crash chest high on your body, Charlie, beckoning me to join you.

St. Valentine's Day

He rolls onto his back and opens his mouth skyward
as if thirsty for rain. I tug off his boxer shorts,
soft, yellow-green, and baggy, He's already hard
Sex can sometimes be a chant that courts
the sun to return, though of course day will come
again anyway, whatever we say or sing. But touch,
or rub his knees, the scratches on a thumb,
his few chest, thick pubic hairs, sinewy thighs, then clutch
his body boldly, tightly with your arms as you kiss
him, his kiss back bright as an angels' tongue
of flame, lick the lines of his hands, neck, what is his
what is yours now, sweating together as body plunges
into body without risk of drowning. We wipe each other
off with a towel, pull up the sheets, try to sleep close together.
It is our first night as lovers. Remember this, I urge myself. Remember this.

Three months later, in Ventura, during the Ojai festival,
after an evening of Ives and Stravinsky in the shell,
on a clear night, he and I shower together in a small
stall we barely fit in, scrubbing slowly. It is hard to tell
ourselves what it means to wash each other's chest,
back, butt while the hot water pricks our skin red
as we press deeper, harder against each other, blest
by such closeness. Coming, we groan, sigh, my head
on his shoulder as our seed streams onto the shower's
floor, twirling, whirling round the drain like soap
foam or run-off flowing into gutters after a storm. Hours
pass like seconds when you're making love. Surely hope
is sexual, too, when it's ecstatic. A full moon rains on our bed.
Our sheets are shiny as a scrim. The room looks wet as crests
of waves from the light pouring in and over us like restless, rising rivers.

Throughout life, people may recall the past like runes or fragments
of memories, like sacred scriptures or marks inscribed
on dried hide or chiseled in stone. A few may be laments
of course, but more often they're hymns to a glorified
god, though whom or which no one can know for sure,
though Eros is high among them. When passion makes
itself known, it is like an epiphany, able to endure
only briefly on its own until it's lost like shells the sea takes
back to itself or like images, emblems, exposed to sun
and rain that slowly fade them. Pretend desire is a text
hidden in an amphora in a desert cave, retrieved only
decades, centuries later, damaged by time. What memories sex
creates. Look at how his blond hair flares against a pillow where I see
him still, his Nordic blue eyes staring at me the first morning before the next time.
It's like reading a rare palimpsest, isn't it?, its shadowy words, his bold, bared beauty.

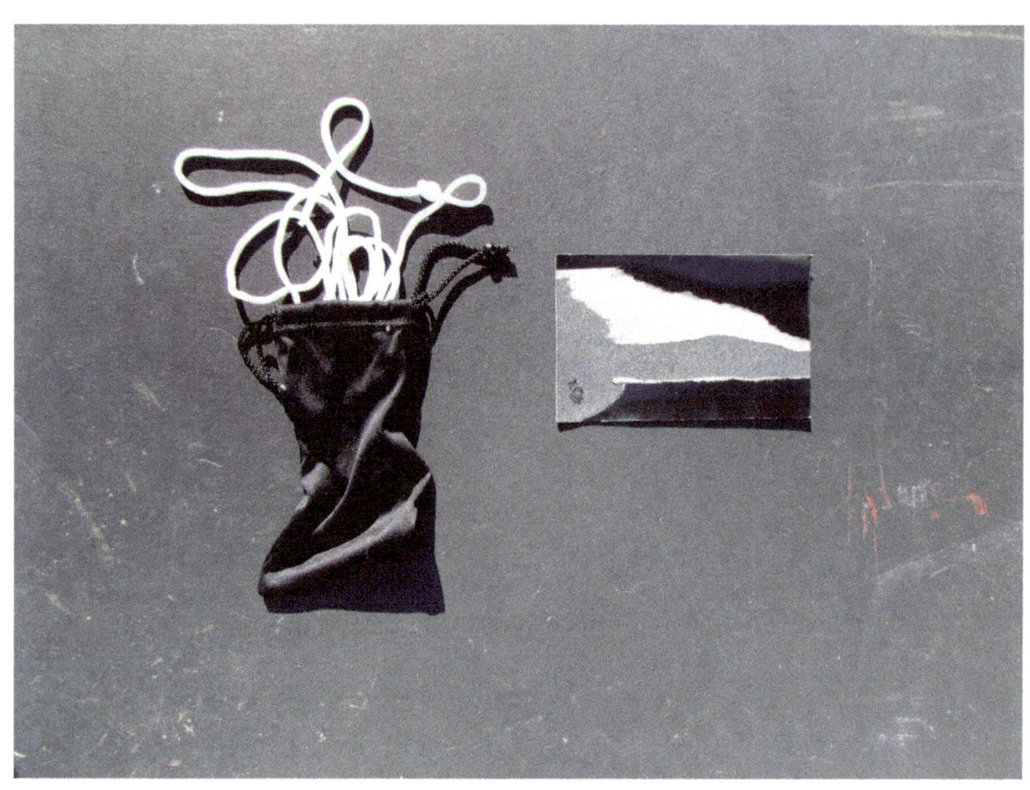

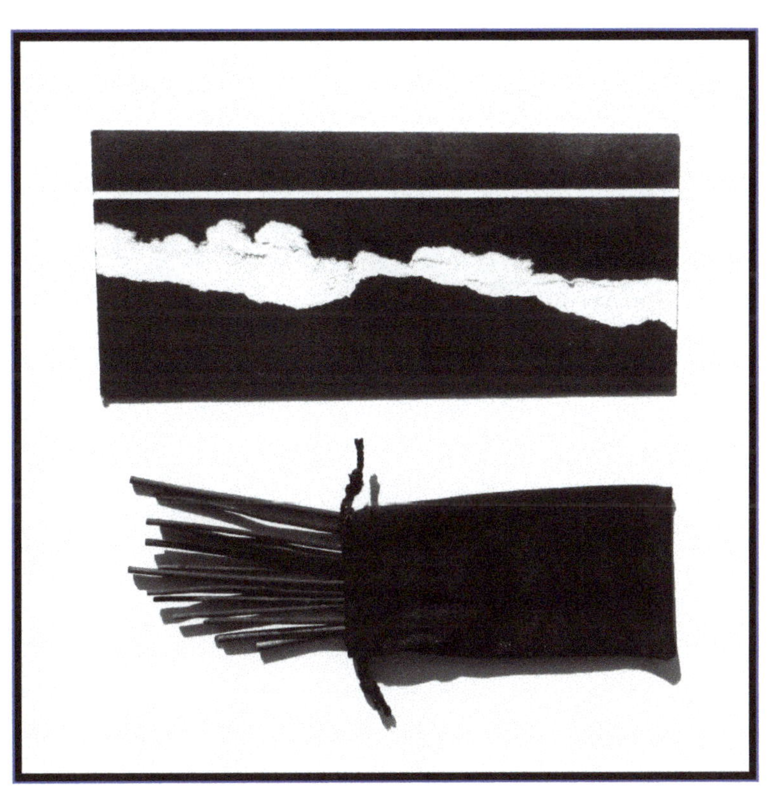

Part V

A Few Old Photographs from Life Magazines

A Lake Country cottage, its patched thatch roof berry
red at sunset. An unbeaten farmer with a scythe felling
wheat in Ukraine. A ballerina leaping in a Napoli
opera house, empty, barren, and dark. A burning
cigarette dangling from a grizzled card player's lips in
a Parisian café, a wine bottle with a candle in it
on the table, his shirt unbuttoned to the waist. A bin
with ice and fresh crab in it on a wharf with a limit
to buy sign tied to it in San Francisco, two sailors
in their Naval whites passing by, drinking beers.
Cliffs by the Adriatic, bombs exploding despite war's
end, shattering rocks and lookouts and three tiers
of fortifications. And see, there's you, anonymous
too, packed in among an enormous crowd in New York City
celebrating the victory, everyone cheering and waving
and laughing and hugging one another as a rain of confetti
falls upon them, and you, only you, whoever you are, bare-
headed, happily staring elsewhere, waiting for something more marvelous
to happen beyond the frame of the photograph, unseen by us, unknown to history.

After Balanchine's La Sonnambula

Midtown, blackout, shades drawn, curtains pulled tightly
closed because of war fears and yet Anina
stands high above all those curious people intently
staring up at her as they would gape at any phenomena

similarly inexplicable or uncanny, rudely startled awake by
policemen's shrilly blowing whistles and the chiming
church clock lugubriously proclaiming midnight. With a happy
little sigh, Anina sashays flirtatiously, lifting her skirt while climbing

each wispy cloud as easily as ball room stairs. In the glare cast
by floodlights, she smiles, her loosened hair luminescent, shining
like the moon whose light she crosses like a bridge, the past
below her, heaven not far above. "How dare you," her mother

snaps. Her father orders her, "Get down here." But her lover
exclaims, "Dearest, I believe you," while she, like a great dancer,
glides through the sky executing her point work so gracefully she
is still celebrated years after as the balletic mystery and comet-like wonder

who shone over New York City during the forties of the last, credulous, tragic century.

At the End of Time

after a fragment for Pound's Canto CXV

He stinks, reeks of where he's been, who knows
for how long? It's hard for him to see clearly,
the salty air stinging his eyes as it blows
off the sea, blue and gently lapping. He must be
a frightful sight, maybe a bit pallid and wormy
still despite his miraculous resurrection, or so
he assumes it must have been. Why else would he be
here and not lying among his fellows in a burrow
or pit of a kind all crowded together and quiet
and lost while they sleep. And then the incredible
happens and stands before him and takes his hand
and brings him back here to speak of it later. Feel
my wounds, it pleaded, feel my sufferings and understand.
So it is with every man and woman.   Believe or don't.
How could it matter? The light will rise at dawn, fail at sunset
anyway. And death's darkness will either consume you or it won't.

Now he is hungry again for honey, dates, figs, the pleasures
of mellow wine, for music, company, good
talk, and an end to solitude. Yet nothing assures
him he'll know how to satisfy his thirsts. Even if he should
find his old friends, who would trust him? Neither
living nor dead, he dwells in the in-between country
of inveterate exiles, his face always gaunt with the gravity
of the grave that as he lay in it never assuaged his hunger
for life, nor its dreams. Why is that? Out of the tumult of rebirth,
he waits alone along the Galilee, restored to the earth
he prayed to walk on once more, wearing his shroud like a shawl,
aware he is only a poem, a fable, the strange gospel story

he's telling to himself, soon to many others, he hopes. Time is not all
there is to life. (These are the words he heard spoken.) Carry
the burdens you bear from your dying with you. Here, by the sea, arise
into language. Love. Do not move.   Let the wind speak. That is paradise.

Eight Love Sonnets
For Atticus Carr

1.

In the Asian Museum each visit, we made sure to study
the cloisonné butterflies and scarlet finches
stitched like light on a gown and the sea
in a scroll beside it painted as if a breeze
were softly wafting over the water while
clouds bathed the coast in sun-rise gold.
You grasped my hand and fell silent, a smile
broadening on your face as you looked that told
more surely than words could of your happiness
at being alive in such a world and led me to remember
the two dozen or more stargazer lilies you gave me
that seemed to be luminescent in their darker-
than-night porcelain vase, emitting a scent so tellingly
sweet it filled the room with your beneficence and kindness.

2.

At mere sight of you, Sappho wrote, my voice
falters, my tongue is broken The mist is sun-lit
this morning, the Pacific mottled, sod-green,
streaked with yellow, strewn with seaweed it
tossed on the beach last night. So I've seen
it for many years now. For how much longer, the choice
is not mine to make. Robbie's snout rests on
your thigh as you drowse. Despite the light shining
outside curtained windows, our house remains
dark until we open the draperies to a late sun
that won't fade books, CD cases, photographs, paintings.

The pleasures that pass between us each night gain
more meaning as we grow older. You are still reading
your book as I walk our dog, the air chill and salty, comforting and unsurprising.

3.

At the Asian Museum, we read the legend about how
the crane of the heart flies toward the sun
to burn illusions away. Below it, the doors of the House
of Pleasure always stay open. Below it, streams still run
toward a river where they flow in a common course
toward the sea. Two men sit by a quiet lake, their row
boat tied to a dock and recall a night together
when they drank wine until there was no more left to drink
and drunkenly watched by lantern light the fishes glitter
like starlight in the lake where they saw, maybe still think
they can see, two cranes stalking through reeds, disturbing
the water, waves rippling toward the sandy bank where, getting
sleepy, the men rested until, when day broke, the birds suddenly took flight,
headed sunward, as if they were not two but one free of illusions, soaring out of sight.

4.

He tugs out weeds, prunes bushy plants growing
too high, puts in new sod and fertilizer, tills
the soil, waters flowers, humming, smiling
like a child playing a game with trolls,
imagining them alive with tales to tell.
Everywhere in the small yard, gophers dig holes,
eat roots, destroy what they devour, yet dwell
safely underground. It's an endless battle
between him and them they win since he's incapable

of harming a soul. Romance errs when it compares love to
flowers, beautiful and evanescent. What of the one who
tends them daily, watches over, worries about them?
Maybe gardening is his lapsed Catholic way of singing hymns
as he cares for nemesia, salvia, oxalis, peonies, marigolds, mums.

5.

Elusive silence, the mutely meaningful thing
I have tried to hear in the music I
listen to, not what a singer might sing
or an orchestra play but what might lie
silent in the notes, hidden, not sounded
but implied, like a word never said
but spoken anyway, understood yet a mystery,
like someone seen from afar or by failing eyes.
I've told you how I once saw in a rose stem
broken by sunlight in its crystal vase an image
as lovely and calm and wise as an ancient sage,
like a Buddha almost, or as a crèche from Bethlehem
I could believe in as I did long ago, as I believe in love
when it's left untold like anything too important to speak of.

6.

Last night, we embraced as the young do, not
asking more from time than it is willing to give
us, not expecting another July 4th on a hot
night on China Beach, firecrackers, like live
ammunition, exploding around us that gave
new meaning to the holiday as we made love in
a cliffside cave. How long can memories save
us, or shouldn't we ask them to? Are words that begin

in the past able to endure a lifetime? Note them down
in your heart like images from a poem you love so
much, have read so often you've memorized it. Brown
thoughts obsess the old. How much there is left to do,
to learn, to know? It may surprise you I speak of God, Emily
Dickinson wrote, who know him but a little, but witchcraft is wiser than we.

7.

At the Asian Museum, we can't see the screen in one view.
No matter how far back we stand, the mountains, like
gigantic moss-covered pine cones, lean, bent askew
by time and weather, its slopes too sheer to hike.
We move from panel to panel. Much is shown in miniature,
minuscule cranes, two men poling two tiny boats
on a river widening where it's fed by streams. Culture
is the past transfigured into stories. A solitary duck floats
on a pond. High up, in a wood hut, two aged men
wearing fluent robes talk while gesturing, their faces
little more than a few quick brush strokes. In a den,
or maybe it's the open mouth of a cave, a monk
sits, contemplating the grace of clouds and a plum tree trunk,
knowing, like the begging bowl he holds, heaven is everywhere he gazes.

8.

A small dog, a brindled poodle mix, lies in the north-bound
lane of The Great Highway, run over or hit.
Cars dash past or attempt to drive around
it. If it's not yet dead, it soon will be if it
isn't rescued by someone. Careless of his safety,
Atticus leaps off the walkway into traffic, picks
the dog up, cradles it like a child, and carries it free
from peril. Its tag reveals its name. The dog licks

his cheeks. The woman who runs toward him saw the harms
he'd faced for her dog's sake. He returns it to her arms
as she cries in gratitude. Life turns into parable. A lost sheep
lies hurt in a thicket among brambles and briars in great danger
of dying from wolves and foxes. A man passes by who would keep
it safe from jeopardy by risking his life. Say he is a shepherd. Call him its savior.

The Guy at Trouble Coffee

Untamed shores, stark mountains, plane trees,
olive groves, grape must, grottos, white cliffs,
plashing oars in shallows, swallows flying,
swallows nesting in his bedroom. Noon
follows noon. Boys in first bloom leap bulls,
run wild, naked, their hair shining brighter
than gilded marble statues, boys who cast
no shadows. Eastern clouds loom low over first light.
The rocky drab hills look like sets for a fate-fraught tragic play.

The past transforms silence into sense, a mythology
of souls, how they change as the wind blows,
why bodies shift as spirits leave them, or new
ones move in, these unstable islands, squalls'
voices, sighing trees, clashing tides, din of waves:
all he's transfigured by as the tan guy, fanged python
tattoos on his arm, his eyes bluer than any sky's
ought to be, stares out the cafe's plate glass windows
past breakers toward a surfer's dreamed of unmapped beaches and seas.

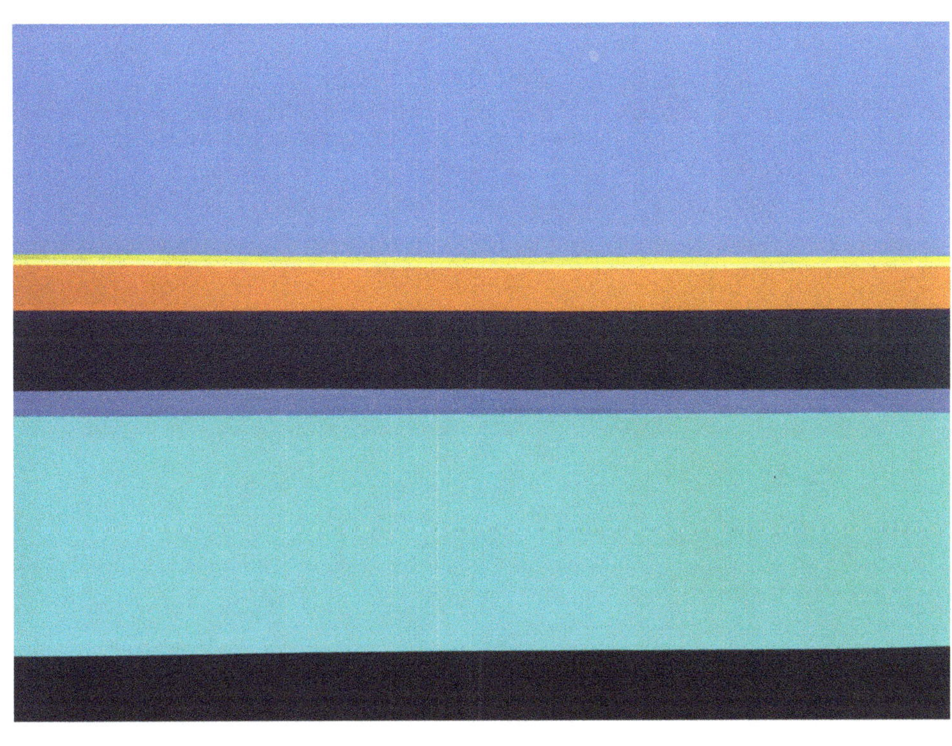

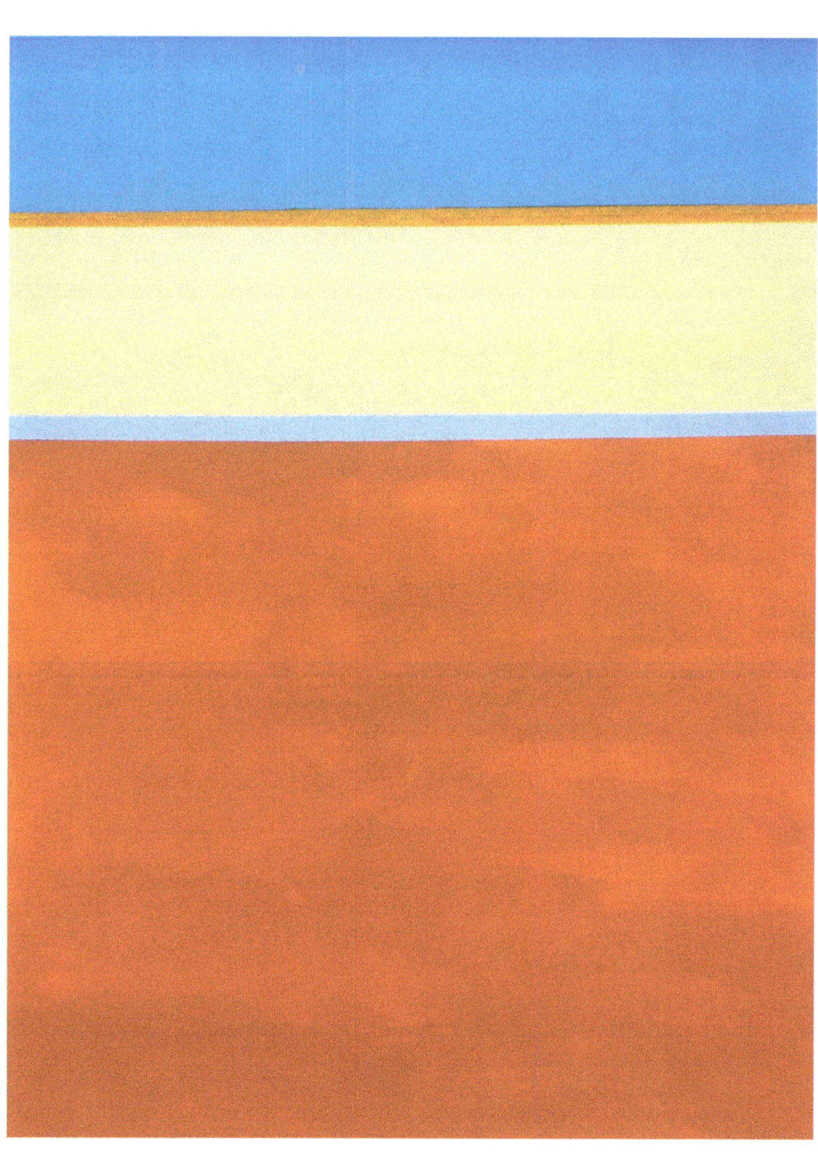

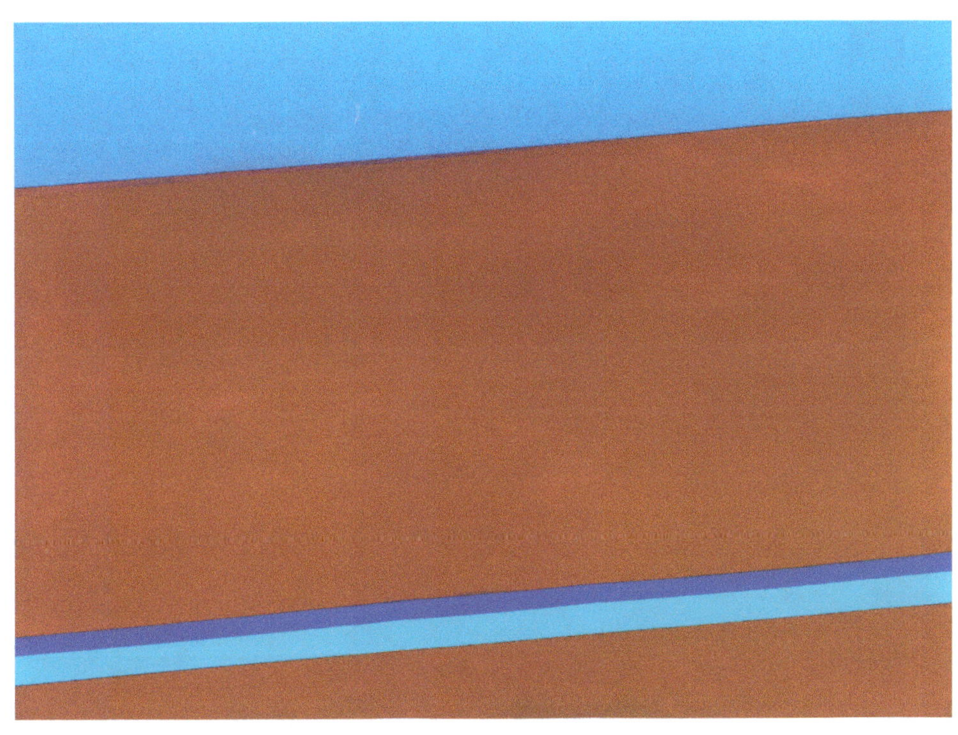

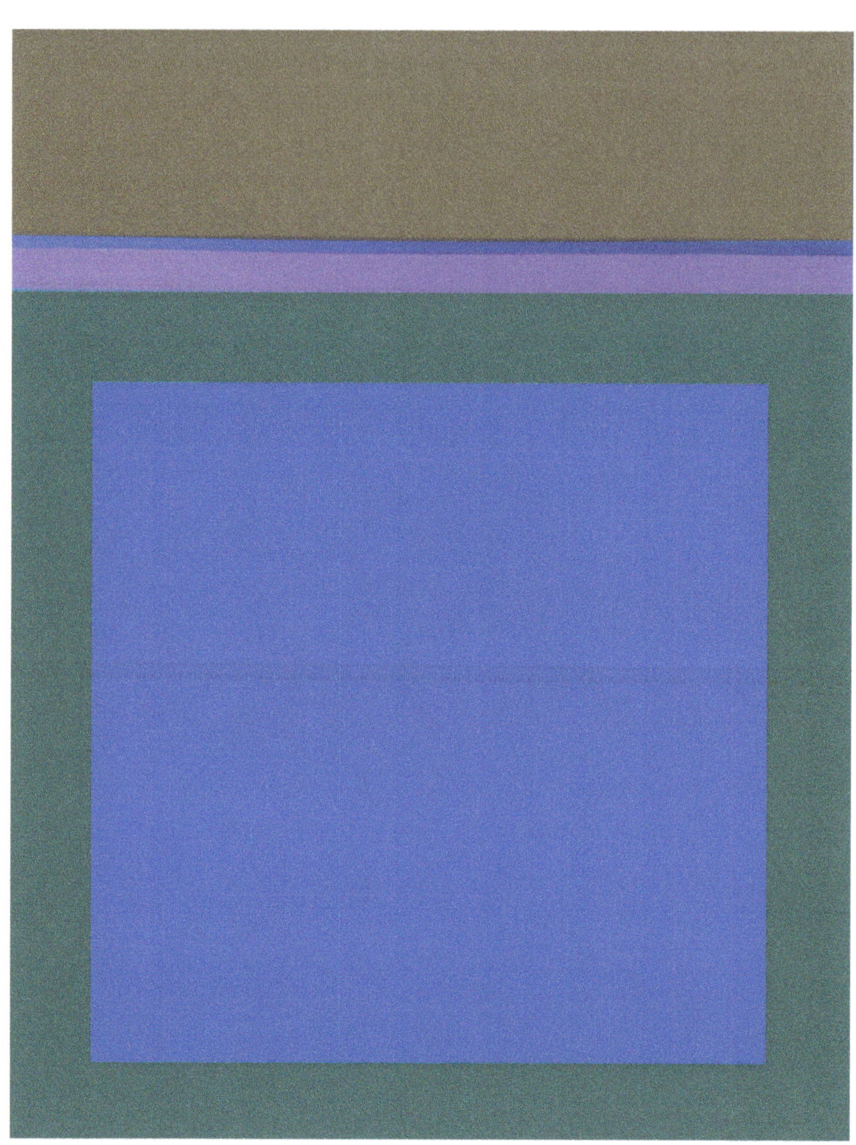

Book II

Part I

Gerald Coble, 1932-2021

Throughout his life, Gerald Coble was devoted in his art to two obsessions: landscape and memory. His earliest work, from the late fifties and early sixties, were paintings of the Carolina fields, woods, and lakes near his cottage and studio outside Greensboro and the seascapes off the coast of Ocracoke Island in winter or Cape Cod in springtime. Like many artists then, he had been deeply affected by the new American art of the mid-century, at Black Mountain and in New York City, especially its calls for art to return to the essentials of its vision.

For Gerald, that meant, above all, a vision of sky and earth and light seen joined together in a work approaching abstraction but never altogether eliminating the "world" from his painting. He was particularly interested in how color evoked reality especially at the dividing line, the horizon, that dominated much of his work.

When Coble moved to Manhattan in the early sixties and began to live with his lifetime partner, Robert Nunnelley, a former assistant to David Smith and an important painter as well, he began to draw a lot, mostly in ink on large sheets of paper, figurative work, often male nudes, meticulously, scrupulously drawn. After he had spent over a year in Italy, near Volterra among other sites, history, images from the past entered into his graphic pieces, ruins, sculptures, and over and over throughout his lifetime, images drawn out of or referential to Botticelli's Primavera.

After, in the early seventies, he and Bob had moved to Battenville into their early eighteenth century home along the Battenkill in upstate New York, Gerald began to make collages, combines, sculpture, often uniting found objects stilled into a single image by the simple act of framing. For example, in one piece, a century old boy's shirt is shown hanging from a wire hanger with a black mourning band wrapped around one sleeve. Or, in another, an antique Sicilian door he'd found is left as is, but surrounded by a worn, gilded frame. Postcards, threads, spools, cut out images, photos, pencils, feathers are mingled with gestures, additions he has made with paint and ink or pencil, the hand of the artist also present. In all these images, the past is inescapable, elusive and yet ever present.

For almost a decade or more, he made few paintings. He assembled perhaps hundreds of collages, small and large, for example of a single pyramid and its shadow. He was pondering fundamental images reduced to their essences and the potential for evocation, for otherwise unseen meanings, when so stripped down.

But, later in life, he embraced painting again, as if, in a way, returning to where he began some fifty or sixty years before, looking at the fields and brown-red clay and fine, bold skies and strict horizons of his early life in Carolina. These late paintings are, like much of his work throughout his life, about essences. That which exists through itself as translated by an artist's vision is what is called meaning, one might say. The surfaces are flat, spare, almost bare at times, yet, through color, they all emit an inner light. In this they acquire what might be called the genius of a late style, the genius of simplicity.

The two greatest influences upon Gerald Coble's life's work were not painters but Marcel Proust and Igor Stravinsky. In them, he found the sense he needed of the artist's ethical responsibilities to form and the aesthetic ones to the enduing presence of the past, both, after all, like him, creating their work not only out of personal memories but the memories retained and sustained by what we call history, a history which is not merely a written record but an ever present presence for those who can see or hear or feel it. Varied as it is throughout his long life, all of Gerald's work is united by a single vision: landscape is memory, memory is landscape. Place and time shine and make their shadows together.

What an artist tries to accomplish, he believed, is to show that unity: form and transience, the enduring and change are conjoined, married, in the aesthetic order, the made thing, the work of art. That is the joy of it. But it is also its sorrow. In Le Temps retrouvé, Proust wrote, "Les vrais paradis sont les paradis qu'on a perdus." The true paradises are those one has lost.

McAdoo Farm

Real life sometimes begins surprisingly, the way
paradise might come out of nowhere, from nothing
but the ordinary moment, like the world as it is on a day

when the sun is also young, its golden morning
hiding behind trees, hickory, pin oak, and pine,
as a boy drives on Westridge Road, listening to Elvis sing,

past ranch houses and a few last farms, the shine
of dawn brightening as he enters the battleground,
waving at the statue of General Greene on his equine

mount, its unpolished patina mossy and browned
as the fields where for centuries soldiers have lain.
He turns right at the drive-in theater, heads southbound

on a wooded road, reaches the McNairy domain,
a big white clapboard house, a gentleman's dairy
with a black angus herd where he manages to restrain

from beeping his horn since Walton must be sleepy
from last night's football game. His heart is racing
as the boy pictures Walt lying in bed. He passes slowly,

stares at the windows, speeds up where the fencing
ends and the lake begins, turns onto Church Street,
and reaches Gerald's cottage at McAdoo Farm. It is spring

everywhere. All is blossoming, May as yet incomplete
with more bounty to come. Ezra, Gerald's stray
mutt, named for Pound because found the day the poet

was released from St. Elizabeths, barks, wanders away
from his offered hand, sniffs weeds, turns round,
looks toward the woods, not interested in play—

untamed, half feral, and free. He watches him bound
over the fallow field toward a long row of cane
and the forest beyond and lowers the sound

of his car radio, though he listens until the refrain
is done—"without a love of my own"—no one,
poor guy, then clicks it off, his teenager's pain

that no one must know, his secret, as heavy as a stone
in his gut. He knocks on Gerald's door. More music.
What piece is it? Why does music let him feel less alone?

A George Arnold hangs over the couch, Antarctic
inspired, two bands, sky, land, the upper part blue,
the lower ones reds and oranges, no impasto, nothing thick,

but transparently brushed. In the studio, the work is all new,
Gerald's recent paintings on his floors and walls,
strict horizons, pointillist foliage, calligraphic lines, a few

in casein evoking pebbles in shallow brooks or waterfalls
splashing on granite or searchlights scanning a runway:
all landscapes. Vocation, the boy's dad says, is whatever calls

you to make your life real. But the kid has nothing to say
of his own, can only imitate, pretend to be
whoever he is mimicking, like a radio deejay

mouthing the words to a hit '45. He can see
only what he has been taught to see, a chameleon,
or what is worse, a chameleon cliché, not really free,

whose colors match whatever branches it stands on
as it waits for the morning sun to warm its blood,
lizard-uncertain if it will survive to greet the next dawn.

Only others' eyes can show him, let him know what's good,
like Gerald's as he patiently watches him paint
in a different style each Saturday morning. It is understood

he will play records, not talk. The boy's musical saint
is Berlioz, but today Gerald chooses Shapero's
Symphony for Classical Orchestra, not a faint

Stravinsky rhythmic rip-off or a grim Schoenberg minus tone rows,
but Haydnesque in its wit and gentle melancholy.
The boy's enjoying it more each time it re-plays. It shows

in his work, Gerald says, grabbing his shoulder. "See?"
And possibly he does see, in the particular blue in his sky
with too much earthbound, lichen green in it to be

the less real one gleaming outdoors. He doesn't ever mean to lie.
Maybe he does look deeper inside, yet further below
he fears there is nothing to see, just dark, too scared to reply

to the warmth of the love in Gerald's hand. He does not know
what to say, how he should feel or respond. Gerald removes
his grip, sits on his low marble checker-top table. The boy must go

soon. It is late afternoon. He is paint-spattered, head to toe, shoes,
shirt, jeans. He has his father's lawn to mow,
a date that night. As he leaves, he moves as a shadow moves.

It is too early for him to love, not that he is cold or callow,
just scared of the truth of what no one approves
of in his world when on that day more than sixty years ago
a boy senses in one man's touch the promise of more joys to follow.

Battenkill

It's famous. "Best trout fishing stream in America."
Here, the river doglegs, forming a pool Eakins'
boys would have loved if they'd lived near, flat,
man-sized rocks to sun on, a hemp rope, high
as a silo, tied for years to an old oak branch
still able to support two or three grown men
swinging over the waters, frothy where deepest,
to dive or cannon-ball in. Summer is such
a kingdom on the Battenkill. Idling bird song.
Folks on inner tubes floating by. Beyond Gerald's
and Bob's, it curves past bridge and silent mill.
In the corner of yards, on the border of farms,
headstones stand erect or lie half-buried,
well-kept or moss-covered, some chiseled with dates

older than the Battle of Saratoga. Small American
flags, some wind-shredded, memorialize the fallen.
Its planks peeling like infested redwood, fathomless
pits gaping between boards, a barn forms
a backdrop of sorts to a terrace, one of three
edged by brush and rocks, that descend to the water.
Fenced on both sides by fragments of stele or bits
of monuments no longer standing or long torn
down, its path narrows like an isosceles triangle
to a point where a girl's beautiful head carved,
etched from granite rests on a tall wood plinth.
The woman who posed for it now is dead, lying
only a few miles away under her own stone,
guarded fancifully by giant sculpted dogs.

Memory is a heraclitean flow none can cross
the same, unchanged, each time. I barely met
her, spent much of our one afternoon together
talking Faulkner with her and her husband, saying
how in his art landscape, place, is always part
of us and the past races past us faster than
the future can try to catch up–or something
like that. Who knows anymore? The face she wore
was an old woman's graced by joy like Hals'
Malle Babbe, an owl, wise to age, also darkly
perching on her shoulder, the girl she was
and is in the sculpted portrait still visible, as if
life were endless, streaming like the Battenkill
under winter's ice, struggling to stay river.

From a Letter Gerald Wrote Late in His Life

I can't help but associate Shapero's music with those long-
ago days when his symphony became an anthem of some
sort for us. No work from me. Everything I make now feels wrong
somehow except for sketches on paper of a few gum
and maple trees half bare on the other side of the river.
Bob dislikes talking about art now and wants to hear only Mozart.
Winter and the virus have called attention to our ages, though
he stays abed later more, rueful that he's ninety two. My heart
beats erratically. Hemschemeyer visited and left a copy of her
weighty Akhmatova on the seat of our car with a note. So kind
of her. We were able to sit on the deck and watch the river
and a pair of eagles diving for fish. I am able to write solely on lined
paper these days. Bob likes to talk, when he does, about his forays
into the Cedar Bar back in the fifties. It is a strange time in so many ways.
I hope we can survive it. But I see shadows falling on things I love wherever I look.

Reverberations

As you chatted with friends in the Piazza San Marco
watching tourists while you sipped an espresso,
you heard far off an amateur trio–violin,
clarinet, accordion–performing an Italian serenade
to a small crowd even though, much closer, within
the Basilica, Stravinsky's Canticum was being played.
Just last month, you wrote to me how you could hear
most clearly in that moment its composer's mastery,
his ability to determine from knowing San Marco's architecture
how long to make the delay he scored between movements
last so that the music's reverberations would be sure
to sound throughout its vast spaces and off walls exactly
for the required duration, composing the silence, how it augments
what is sounded before and after it, the way a painting, you'd showed
me six decades earlier, was less what one saw and more what it pointed to.

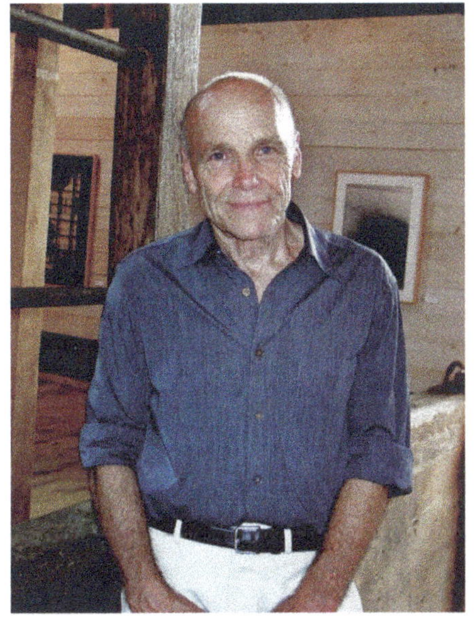

This morning, two days after learning that you had died from cardiac arrest, I read your Battenkill Book 2 once more, ink drawings of a winter river and moon in a series of transmutations. On each recto page, there's a circle, the full moon above, below a rectangle the river flows through. All its verso pages are blank, empty save for the peas, two pods, crisscrossing each other in the lower corners, stamped there as a sign beside an old coin's impress throughout the book. The brushwork is lyrical, calligraphic as poems by Du Mu or Wang Wei. Flowing river and fluent moon seized from the bleak nights of January. What joins us still, Gerald, are love and the wind and water worlds we both chose to live by. Landscape is our book of changes. A painting of yours hangs on my wall, winter fallow fields in Carolina, patches cracked and flaky blotches of white canvas, looking like loss now. All emptiness points to, all it obscures.

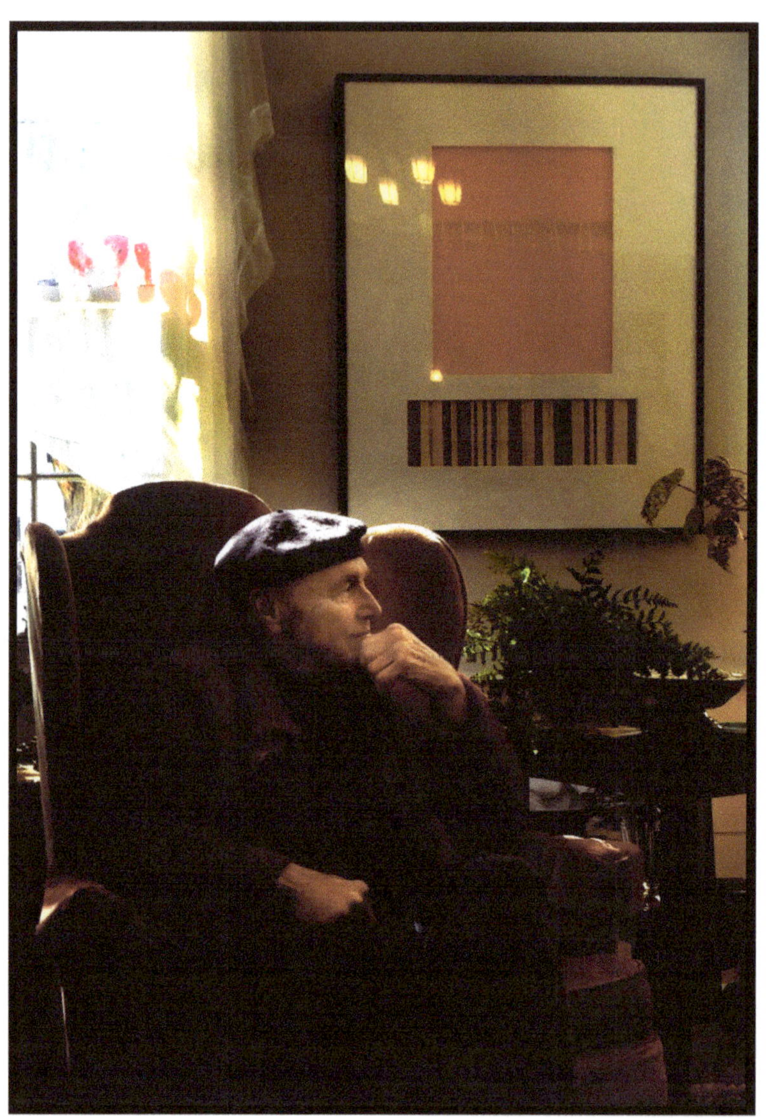

Part II

Afterimages

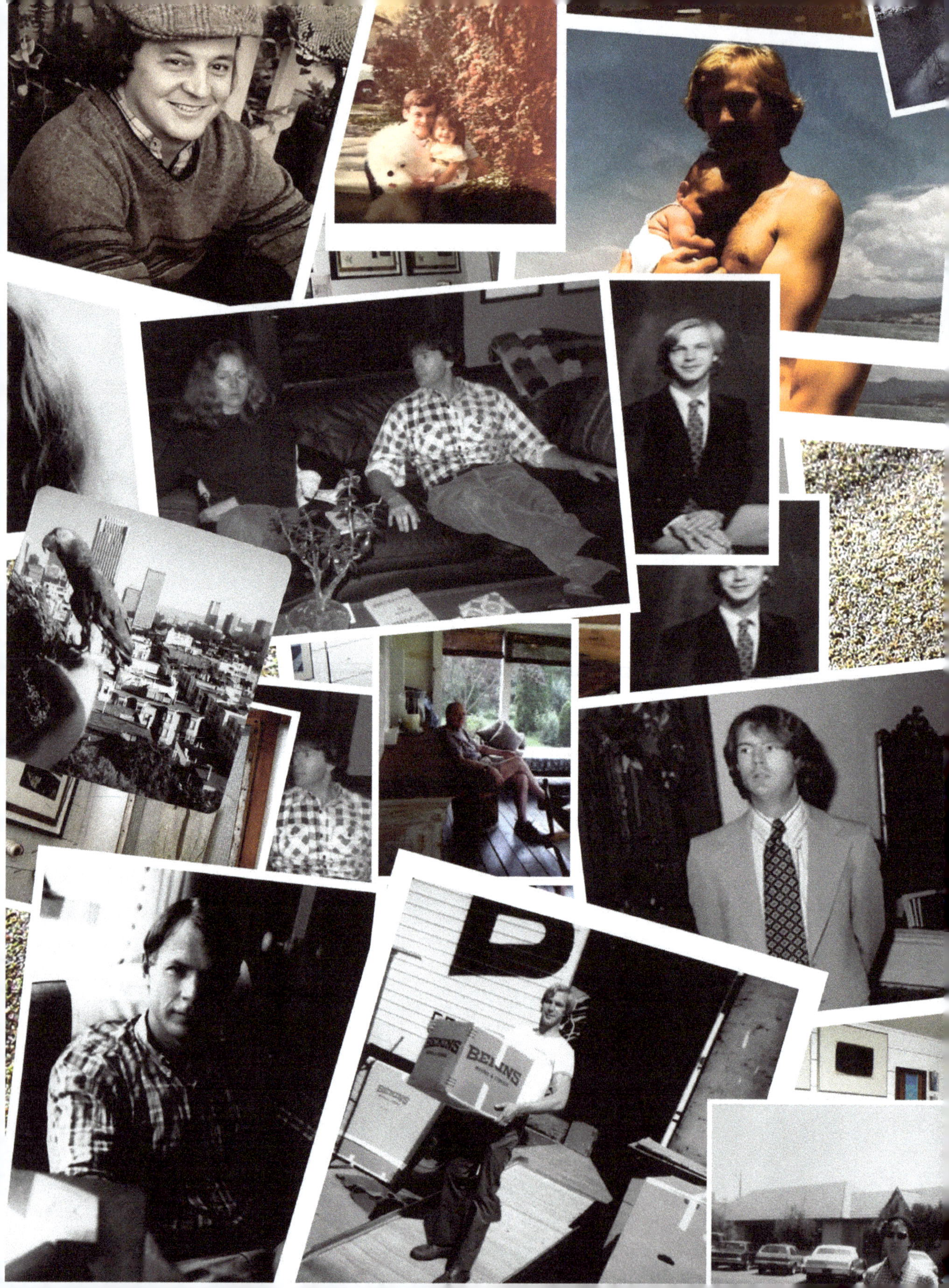

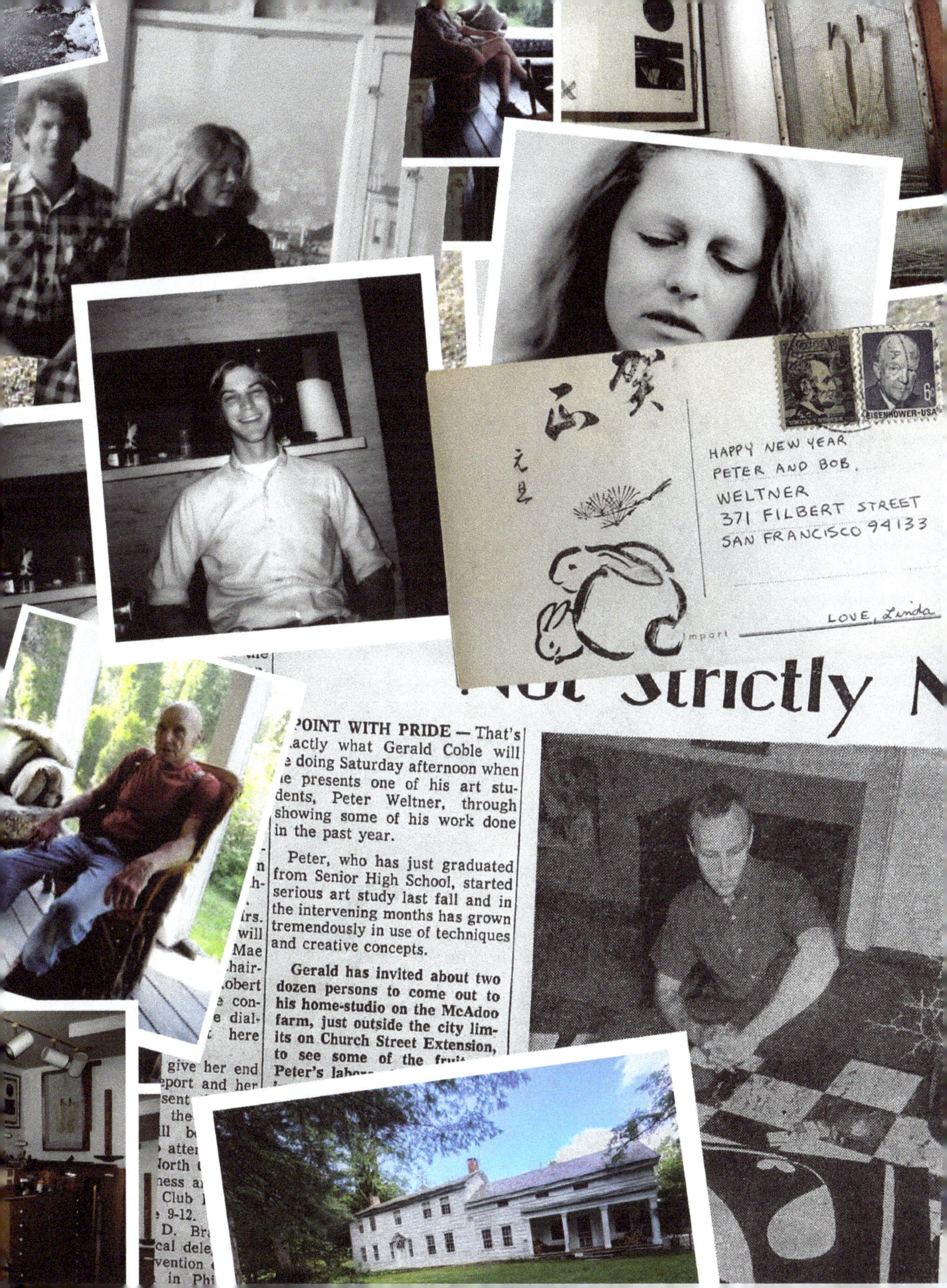
HAPPY NEW YEAR
PETER AND BOB,
WELTNER
371 FILBERT STREET
SAN FRANCISCO 94133
LOVE, Linda
Import
Not Strictly N
POINT WITH PRIDE — That's
actly what Gerald Coble will
e doing Saturday afternoon when
e presents one of his art stu-
dents, Peter Weltner, through
showing some of his work done
in the past year.
Peter, who has just graduated
from Senior High School, started
serious art study last fall and in
the intervening months has grown
tremendously in use of techniques
and creative concepts.
Gerald has invited about two
dozen persons to come out to
his home-studio on the McAdoo
farm, just outside the city lim-
its on Church Street Extension,
to see some of the fruits
Peter's labors

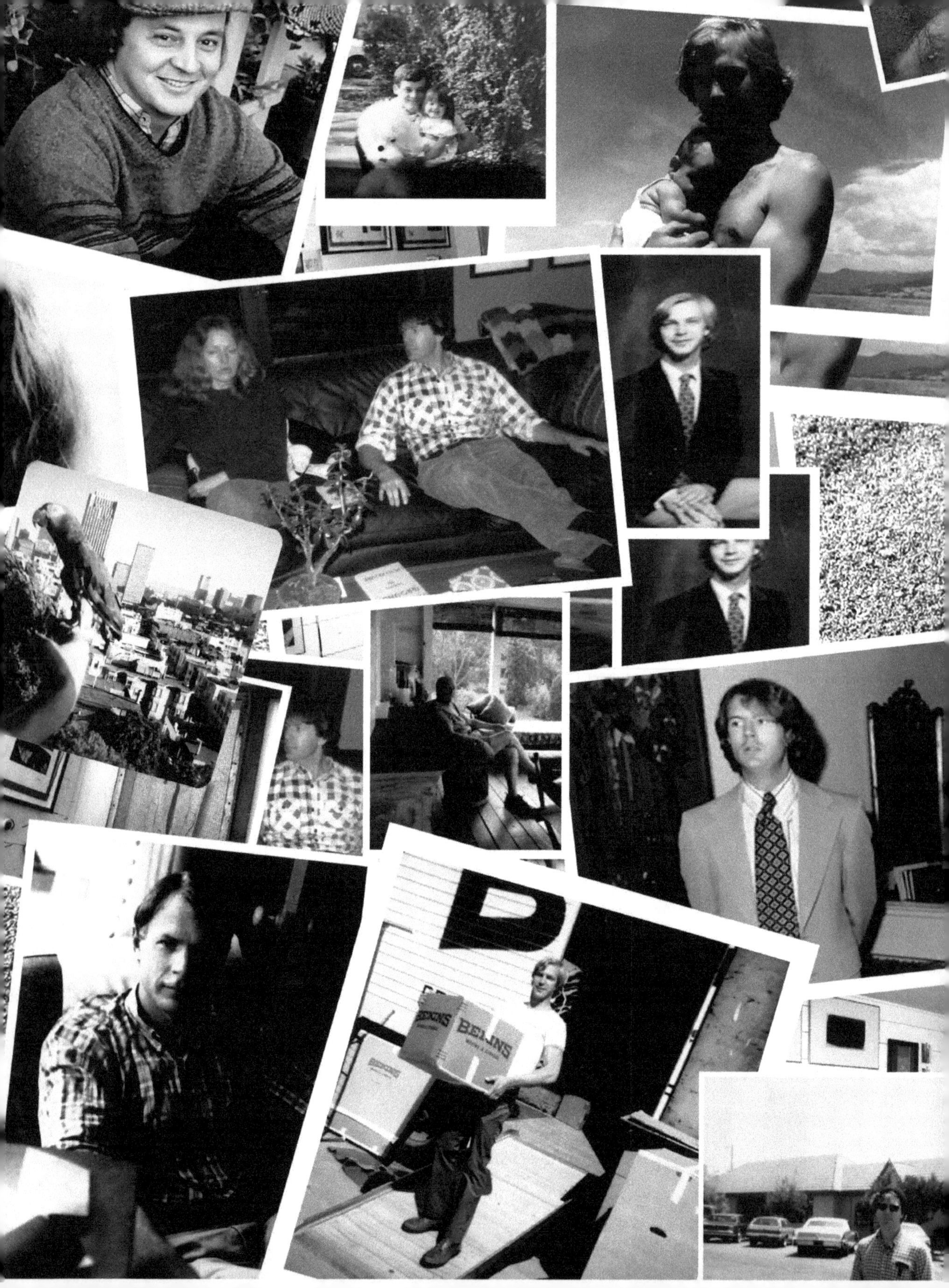

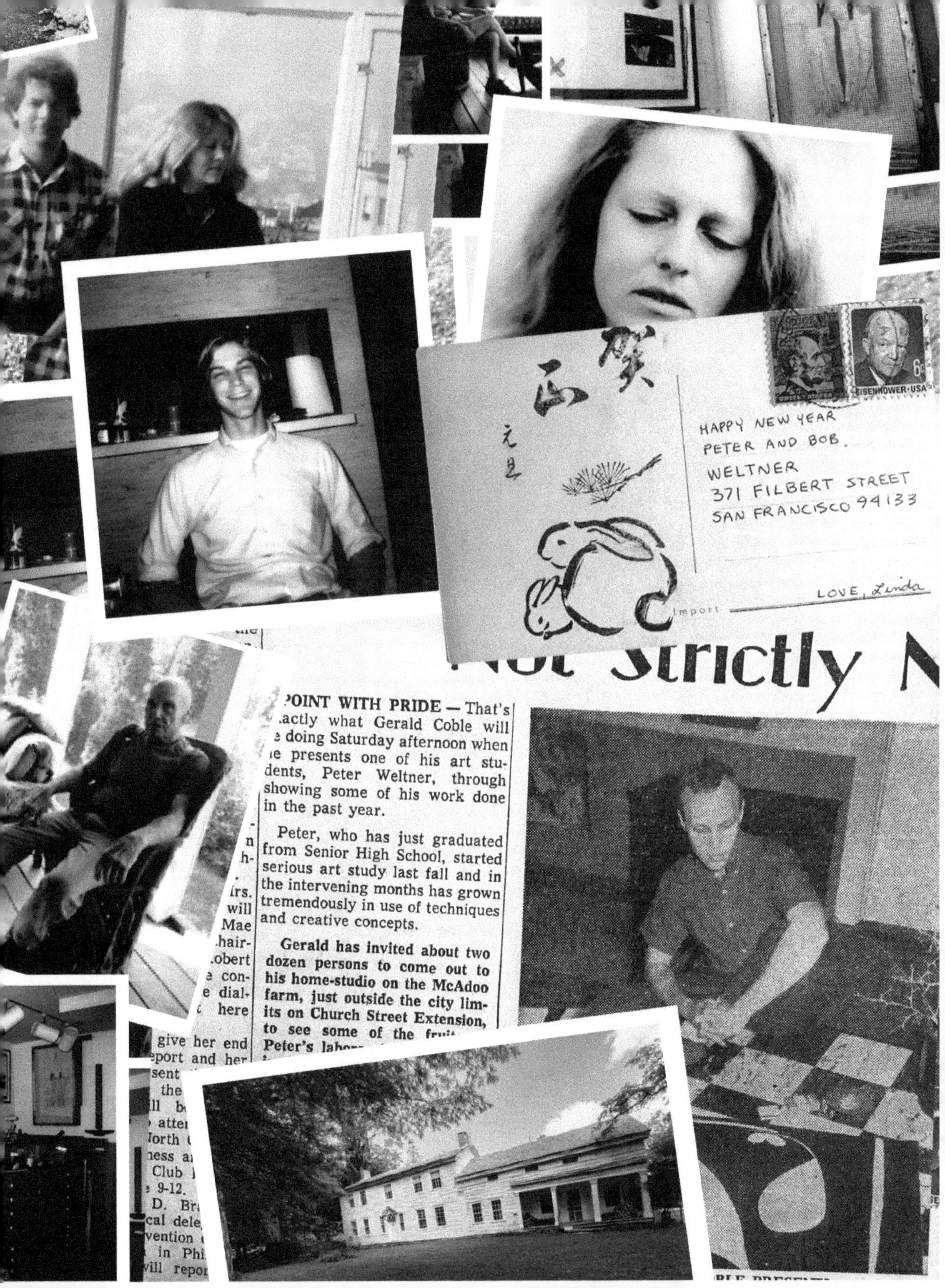
EISENHOWER·USA
6ᶜ
HAPPY NEW YEAR
PETER AND BOB.
WELTNER
371 FILBERT STREET
SAN FRANCISCO 94133
LOVE, Linda
import
Not Strictly N
POINT WITH PRIDE — That's
exactly what Gerald Coble will
be doing Saturday afternoon when
he presents one of his art stu-
dents, Peter Weltner, through
showing some of his work done
in the past year.
Peter, who has just graduated
from Senior High School, started
serious art study last fall and in
the intervening months has grown
tremendously in use of techniques
and creative concepts.
Gerald has invited about two
dozen persons to come out to
his home-studio on the McAdoo
farm, just outside the city lim-
its on Church Street Extension,
to see some of the fruit
Peter's labor

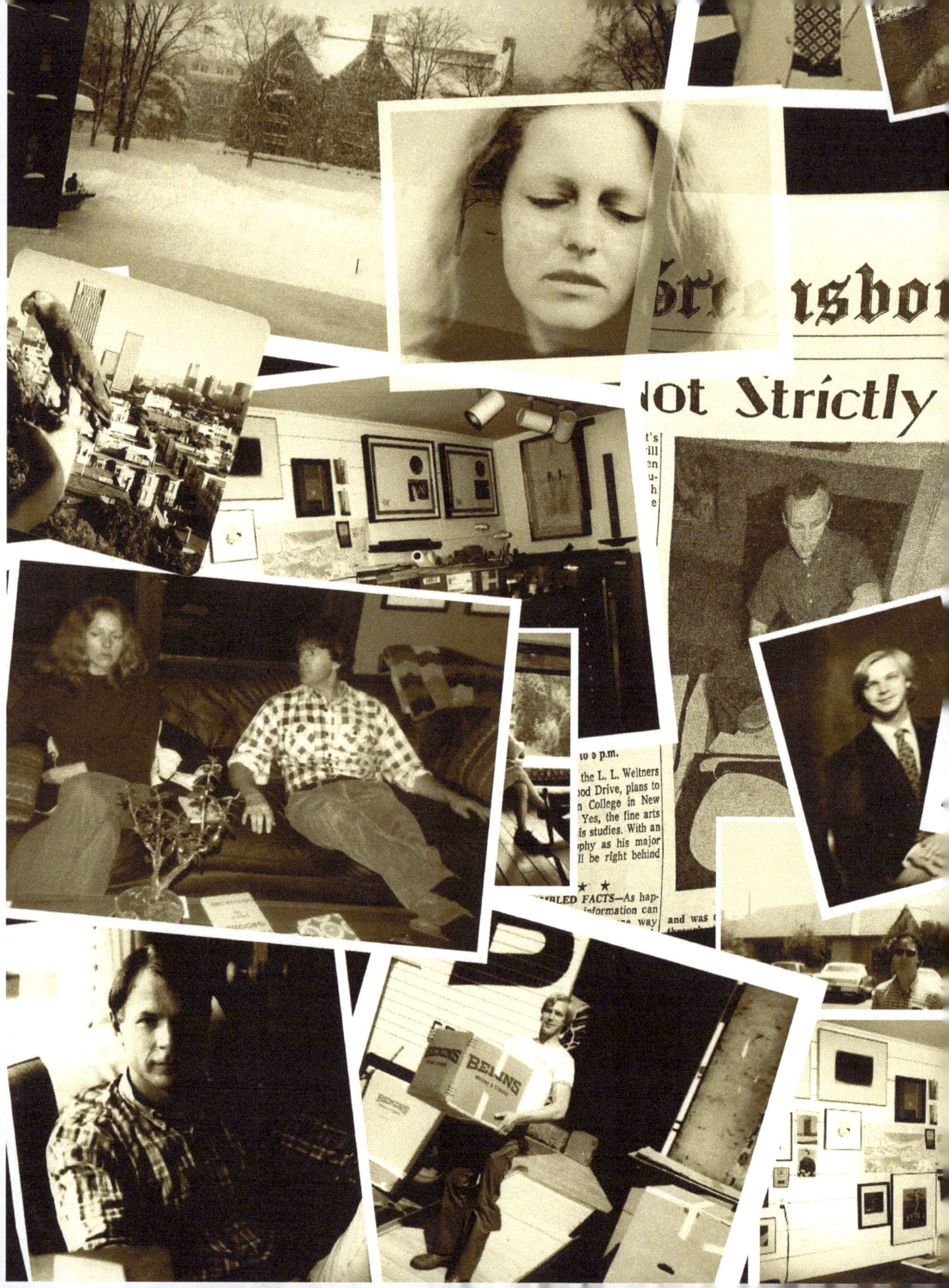
Greensbor
Not Strictly
to 5 p.m.
the L. L. Weltners
ood Drive, plans to
College in New
Yes, the fine arts
is studies. With an
phy as his major
ll be right behind
MBLED FACTS—As hap-
information can
way   and was

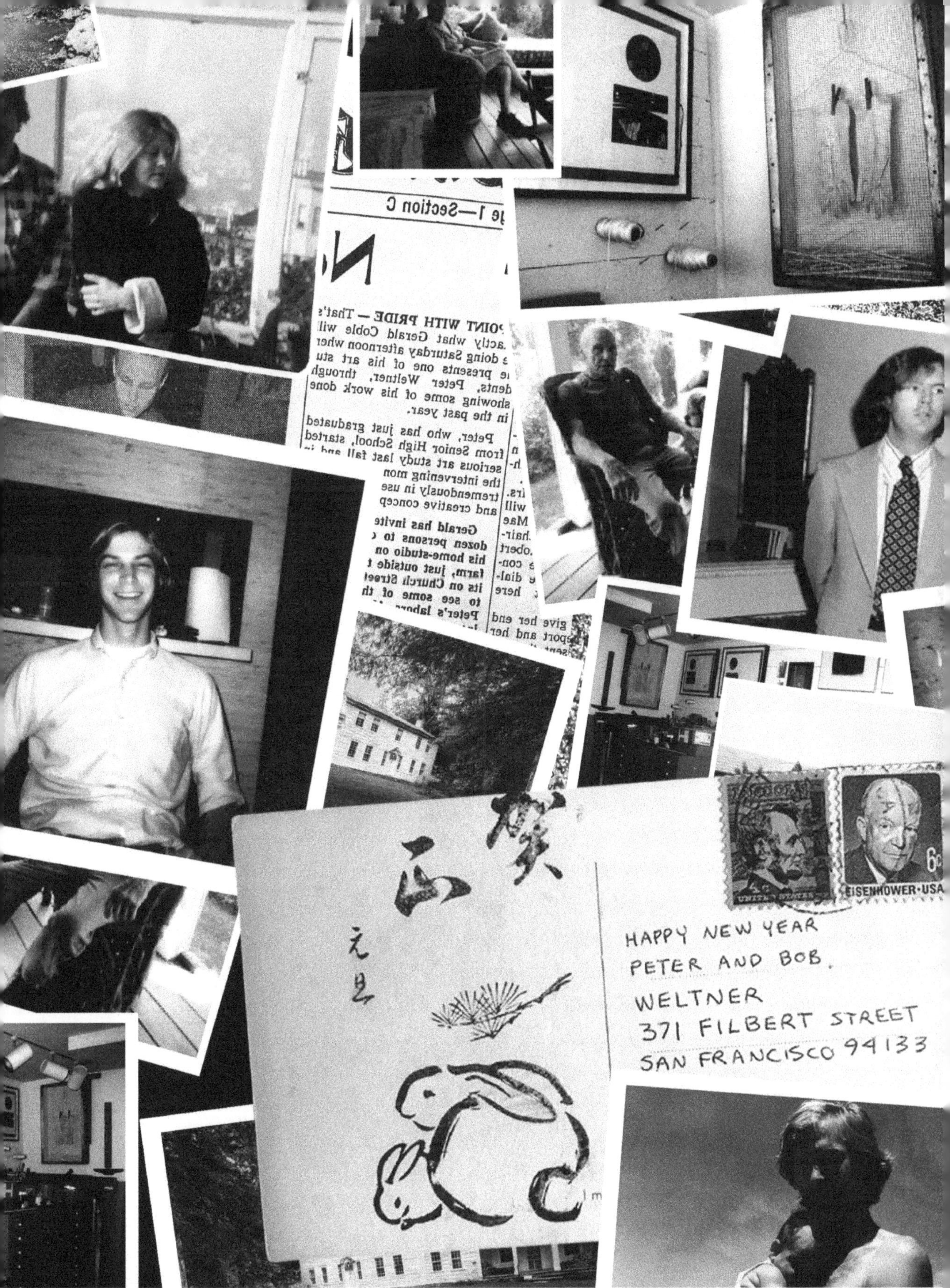
e 1—Section C
POINT WITH PRIDE — That's
actly what Gerald Coble wil
e doing Saturday afternoon wher
e presents one of his art stu
dents, Peter Weltner, through
showing some of his work done
in the past year.
Peter, who has just graduated
from Senior High School, started
serious art study last fall and i
the intervening mon
tremendously in use
and creative concep
Gerald has invite
dozen persons to c
his home-studio on
farm, just outside t
its on Church Street
to see some of th
Peter's labo
HAPPY NEW YEAR
PETER AND BOB.
WELTNER
371 FILBERT STREET
SAN FRANCISCO 94133
EISENHOWER·USA
6c

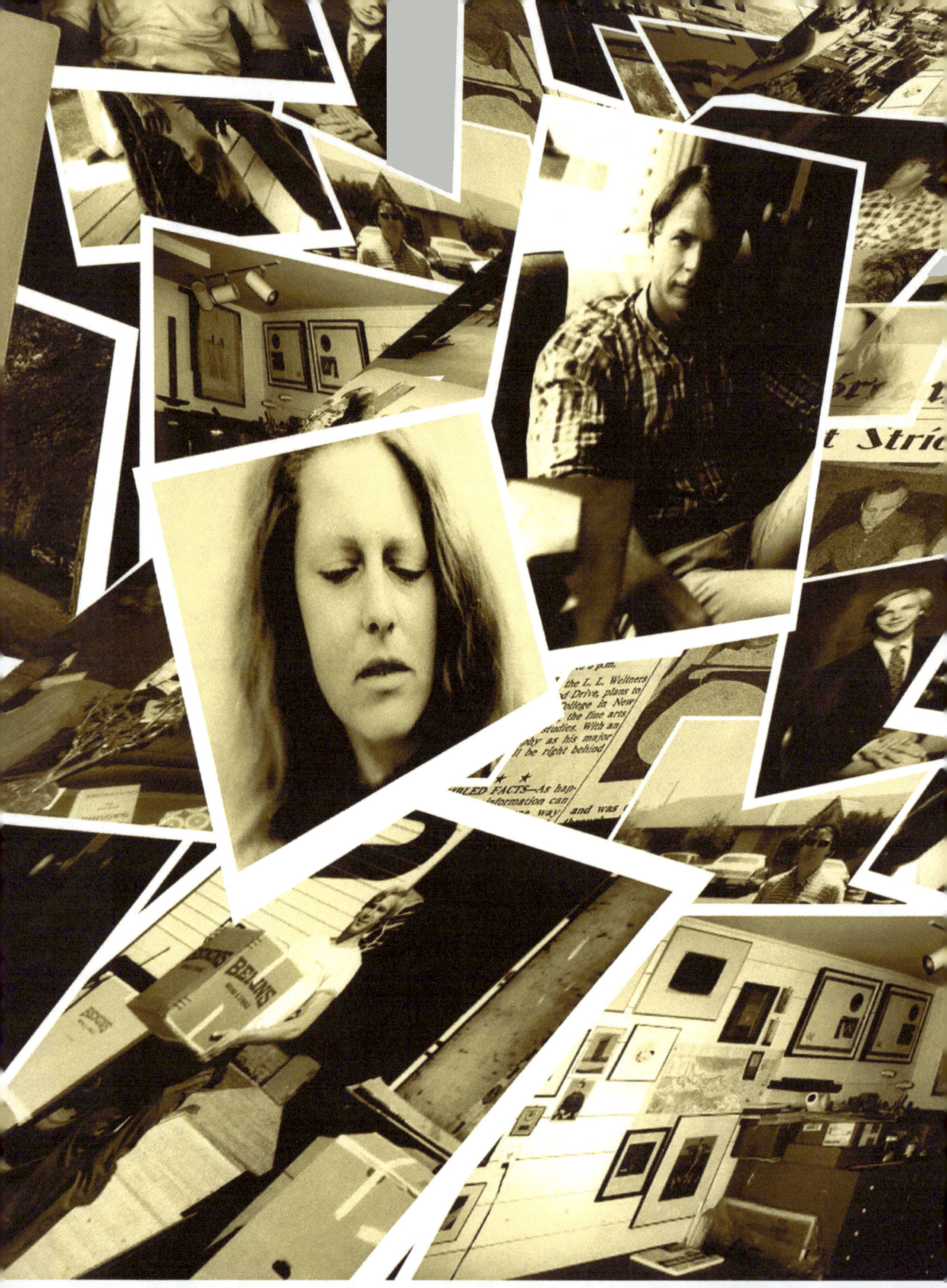
p.m.
the L. L. Weltners
Drive, plans to
College in New
the fine arts
studies. With an
as his major
right behind
As hap-
information can
way and was

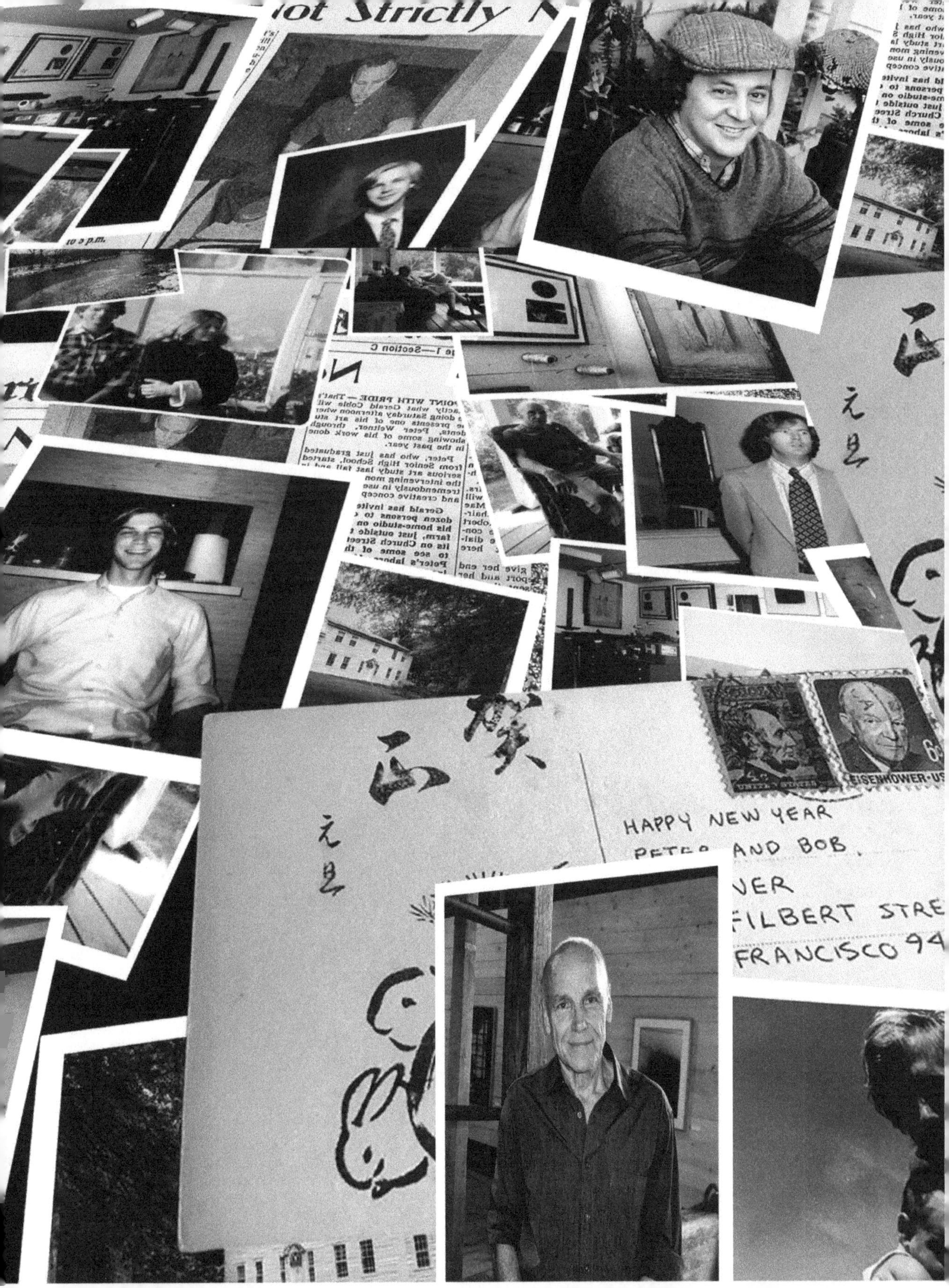

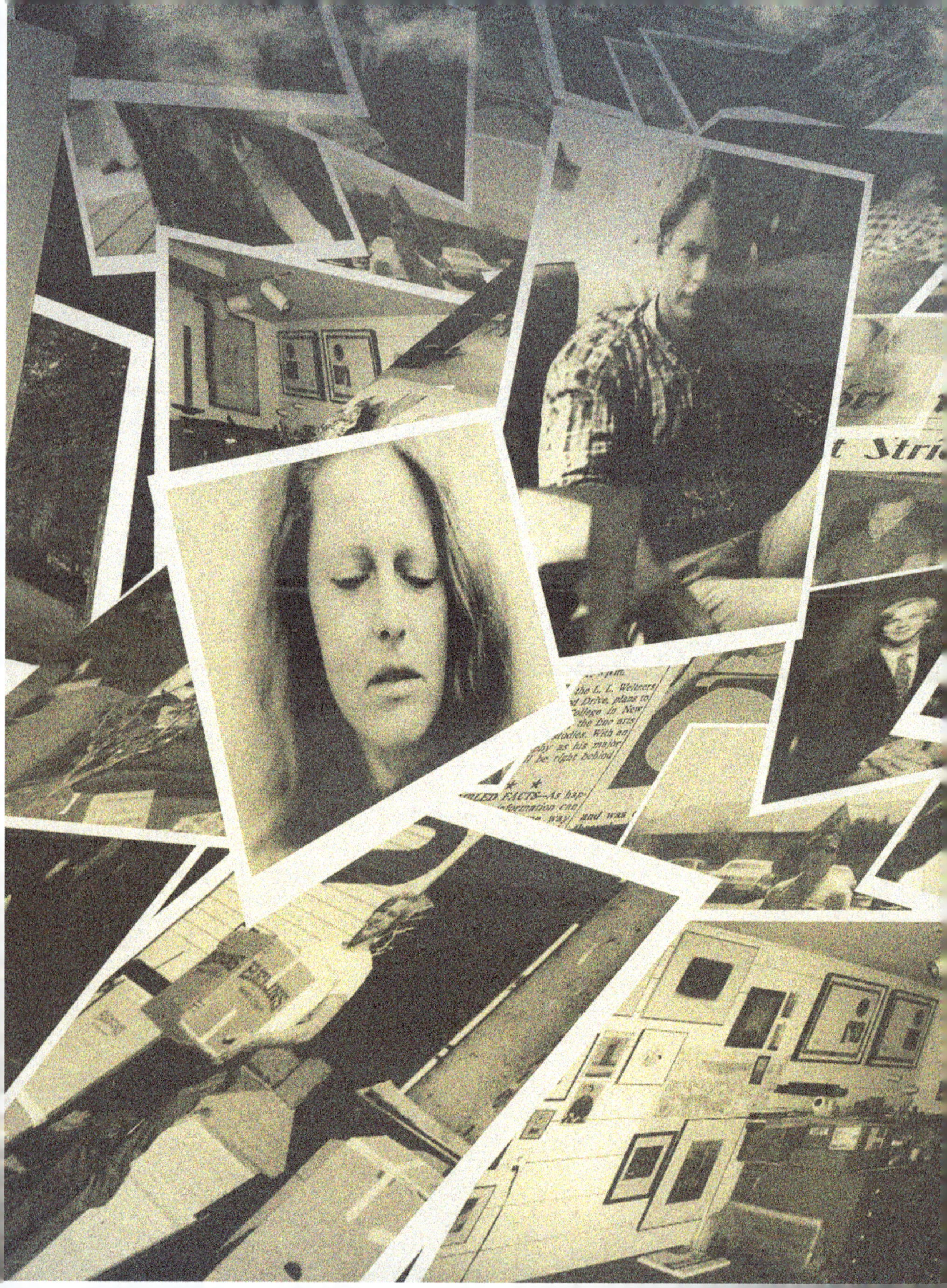

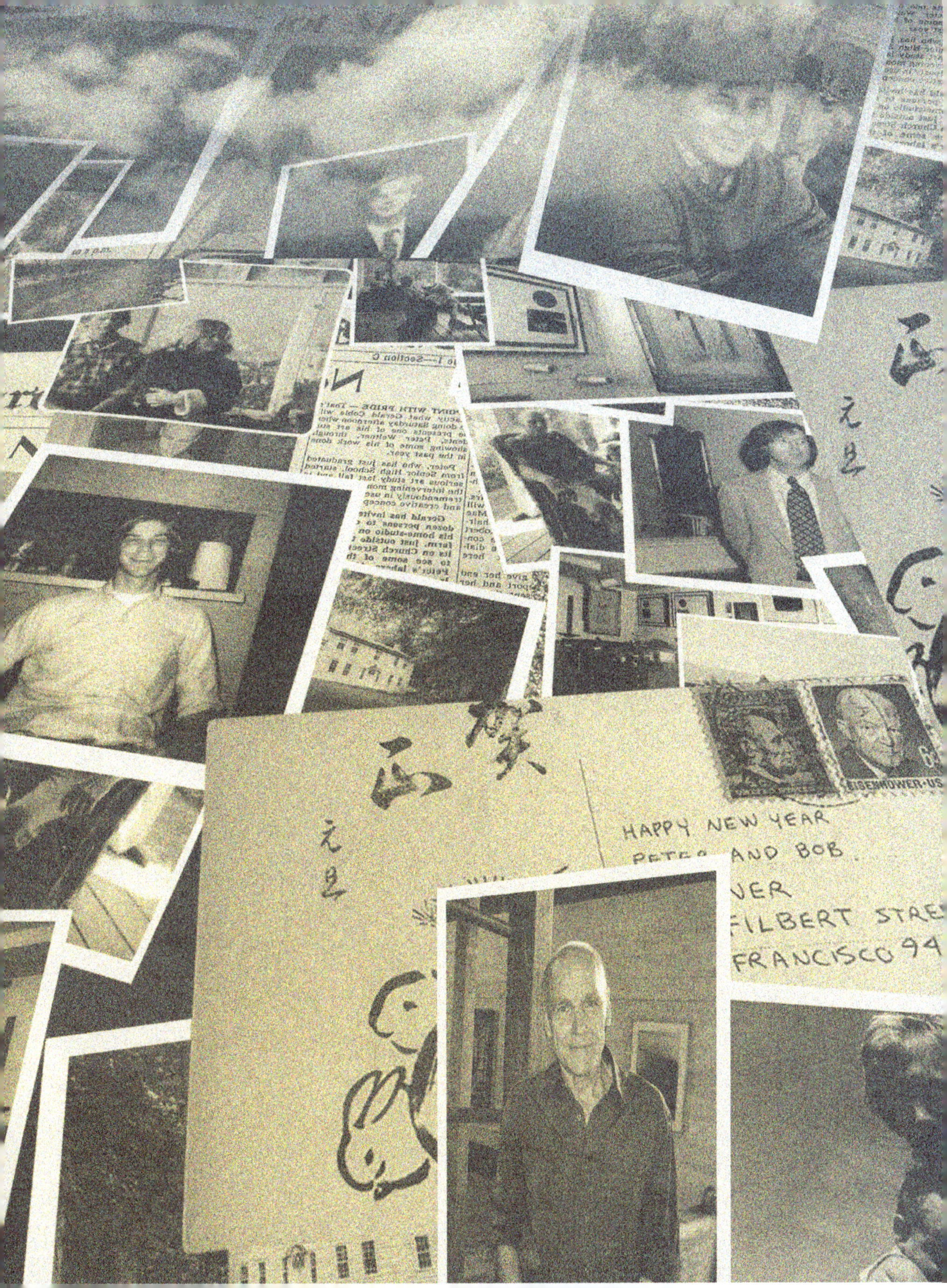
HAPPY NEW YEAR
PETER AND BOB
VER
FILBERT STRE
FRANCISCO 94
EISENHOWER·US

Part III

Marlowe's Passion, after an Unpublished Book, now Lost

I.

1.

A meal and wine shared in Deptford, late at night, the room
lit by a few guttering candles dripping wax
by the bed where he lay in the silence and gloom
of Dame Bull's safe house for agents. Not facts
exactly, though Marlowe, Skeres, Poley, Frizer
were there. It's said an argument about the reckoning
arose that led Marlowe to seize Ingram Frizer's dagger
from him, wounding him in the attack. Fearing
for his life, Frizer, Walsingham's henchman, thrust it in over
Marlowe's wine-reddened eye, two inches deep, an inch wide.
And thus Kit died, a coroner reported. But suppose he lied
to hide what Marlowe might have revealed, testified
about them in court. Spies, double-crosses, assassinations in Douai
and The Hague. Suppose it was not justified homicide, but murder.
Would Marlowe not have said his death was more beautiful if read that way?

2.

Or more stirring as Tamburlaine's ithyphallic rise to a power even he
could not consummate, strutting the world stage
with an artist's authority, victory following victory
in the mounting potency of his self-creating language.
Or more violent like Bajazeth in his cage, braining himself in
desperation, king of kings as he had named himself,
splattering his blood on its iron bars with nothing to win
anymore, everything to lose overwhelmed by the wealth
of Tamburlaine's mounting poetry like an ejaculation repeatedly
delayed. Or more moving like the proud warlord's revealing
his feelings after she'd died, surviving her, his precious Zenocrate.

Or, better, more tragic, like Faustus in Mephistopheles' arms, crying
out, at the end of the play Marlowe might have acted in, ecstatically,
passionately the name of his demon-lover, succumbing to the power
of one he never meant to defy since in their desires, fears, the two were the
same.

3.

Or, far more pitiful, like Gaveston and Edward, Lightborne and the king,
repeating the rhythms of a need that sought through its freedom
the power of an attraction that insists on defeat. Nothing
was their word for the Absolute, their bodies not numb
at the end but on fire with how they would die, the poker
blazing red as the embers in which it was inflamed,
as desire must be red hot to be real, one lover
burning inside the other, like the rod that killed
Edward without leaving a mark on his body, the pain
of it as he cried out, screaming in an agony that filled
the whole castle with his passion: how it should have shamed
him, brought so low by what he had wanted. And Marlowe,
the dagger in his forehead like a burning brand in his brain,
did he feel, in that last thrilling moment, the fate he'd come to know,
like Edward's, spurting, spilling his mind's seed beyond what he'd willed?

II.

All my life, I have watched my king die
in thralls of pain. In this house,
in a room with ox-thick walls,
I have learned the songs of prisoners

while I wait for a lover to strip me.
The air is close. There is no hearth
fire burning. I am dreaming of hounds
by a moonlit pool and the shy gaze

of a boy and the black woods
where I hid as a child in the mild
years after the wars. In the days
before the plague, I made kings

lie in state on stage and cracked
gold heads for food. My enemies
burned with rage. As I gave them
speech, I changed my blood into words

and, with its sanguine pen, impaled
King Edward in the castle's
sink while I clutched pillows after,
sweating through the night.

I've kissed the lips of traitors
and slept with wolves,
the souls of beasts as mean
as men's, though not so cold.

Children haunt me, my poems'
scars, the wounds I've left
on flesh of my soldiers' sufferings.
The stench of human breath

chokes my voice as I cry for my lover
to build a castle, its courtyard
and keep, on my bed, to blanket
it with flowers more lasting than death's.

III.

1.

In many foreign countries, in diverse ways he sought
the secret sympathies in things that grant
a man the gift to create like God once he's been taught
how brute flesh might be made able to chant
like Him, inspiriting lives with the freedom of art.
Call it magic if you like. But why must he become
a trickster of a bogged-down, water-logged hay cart,
of dung-dipped apricots or a plum taste-teaser, some
fool wizard and invisible tweaker of noses, ass-pincher,
parodic artist of belches and gassy bums? He had found words
to blaspheme heaven, God's injustices, and the wrath
to come, convinced he had been damned at birth or like worms
and rats consumed by oblivion. To be forever thirsty for water
or never again conscious of life. There was no other, more righteous path
heaven had given him. Only black dogs barking or cats supping on the brains
of birds.

2.

And yet, "Had wild Hippolytos Leander seen,
enamored of his beauty had he been."
That's by Marlowe. Wave, beaches, love.
The Mediterranean. His dream-spirit keen
on its mysteries, what Neptune saw
in the sea's shimmering mirror above
its currents: not himself, but the sublime
sight of a boy. And the god (the law
of the waters) ordered his horses commit no crime

126

but, as he flung his seed into the sea
only to save him, put "Helle's bracelet
around Leander's arm," never to harm
him or mar his limbs, thighs, chest but let them be
forever embraced by his rolling waters. Why feel alarm?
Many a boy has been loved by the sea, made passionate by sun-borne time.

3.

"But Neptune was angry that he gave no ear
And in his heart revenging malice bear."
So Marlowe wrote in his poem near
the end of his life. Fantasize a moment
with me as my windows shake, the skylight
rattles, waves break, moonlight seeps through shades.
It's another sleepless night, the hours I've spent
re-imagining worlds I've read of until each fades
back to silence at daybreak. I wrote a book, long lost,
on Marlowe. It is strange tonight how ghost-
like it feels to me now, even more as I write
this poem. His poet's quest for an absolute freedom
was doomed to failure, I argued, a fate Marlowe had come
to accept, perhaps, only the moment he died, his Leander,
Hero left alive, unfinished, lovers forever blissful, missing each other.

Eternal Source of Light,

after Edward Hopper, for Galen Garwood

Despite the blank, dour faces of the houses, the ominous,
scary long rows of trees, stark lighthouses, barns,
bleakly Gothic buildings; despite the waiting for a bus,
in spare theaters, rented rooms, lonely restaurants, bars,
the hoping for someone to come, for something
meaningful to happen, the men, women riding on
horseback into a black tunnel with nothing
on the other side of it, with no place else to run
to; despite being aware at the curve by the gas station
the visible world vanishes into once twilight obscures
which way to go beyond the night-solid walls of trees;
despite at the bottom of the stairs, out of doors, each detour
leads only to more obscurity:
                Look. An old man, raking leaves,
pauses his labor for a moment, gazing toward the source
of light pouring, washing over the narrow alley
between houses where he waits, as if he has no choice,
but, daily amazed, to stare at it, hoping to understand
it, that glimpse of reality, before resuming work. A nude,
woman who has just woken up, a cigarette in her hand,
gets out of bed, stands in a shaft of brilliant morning
light that falls through a window like a rite renewed
at every waking, though the sun itself is blocked from her view by
taller buildings. (Maybe she's pondering what the day
ahead might be like if it stays lit like this, softly, luminously
clear.)

And on the Cape, outside the clapboard house they
vacation in each summer, the man sitting, the woman strolling
in hay-high, burnt ochre grass, a couple appears to be straining
to see what their dog, a distracted collie, sees, its keen sight drawn
not to the black dense woods on its left, but far outside the painting
toward the hidden light that on life's daily blessed mornings falls on all randomly
as it offers to all, to their astonishment, the wonder of simply seeing, the freedom
of dawn.

Things as We Know Them

We rarely speak of or write about the loneliness of things,
how sometimes they need us more than we need
them. A teen, I came upon a cabin in woods, weed
and rot infested, rank with decay. What brings
them back to me now, the two young soldiers' photos
pasted on plaster, the ribbon bound, yellowed letters
lying under dust piles on a table (who knows
what they said, the writing having faded away years
before I'd found them), the cracked plates, laceless,
muddy shoes, clay jars that might once have held
creek water, a scrub tub and board, pillow cases,
ripped and torn, smelling of sweat? Who dwelled
there during the war when I was born if only emptiness
inhabited it after? What strangers came later and abused it?

Outside it, the air was gusting strong and warm and quiet,
though I sensed it longed to possess me,
needed me to feel what it feels, see what it can still see,
decades after its family left it, the cabin begging me
not to forget it or deny it's been wracked by pain just as humanity
is when cast aside with the rest of life's discarded, abandoned things.

After a thunderstorm had broken while I watched a moccasin
slither through the rain and battered grass and muddy
red clay toward the lake where I saw it swim in,
I lay down on the banks waiting for the sun to dry
the soaked clothes I'd stripped off and my cold naked skin,
for its light to pour through me as through mist, in that transparent
way I felt whenever I was alone, as if loneliness were meant
to be everyone's, everything's, the whole world's destiny, yet never to know why.

After Shinkei and Wang Wei

1.

He lives alone where no one
dwells close to him in a pine
tree shrine of a kind, a grove
each summer morning tints
a golden yellow, not ignored,
but unadored, an old recluse
some say, like a monk or hermit.
His white hair dangles down,
white knots in his beard
as he ponders if time is an orphan
moon that rises over hills
he has failed to climb or whether
he should let its light relieve
his painful life of its discipline and solitude.

2.

Late age plagues him with diseases.
Illness's birthed twin griefs in him.
He is old. Why does God not let
him die? Night descends, a chill
in the air suffocating him, despair
clogging his lungs like those of a man
drowned in winter below ice sheets.
Blankets, pillows, coverlets, quilts.
There is no end to their number.
Light and dark strangely alternate.
A square block looks the same
as a ball spinning round and round.
People passing by wonder if he is
as good as dead or only mocking their confusions.

3.

Steamed brown rice tastes bitter
as quinine root. He lies confined
to his oak bed, his body scrawny
as dogs in a summer of famine.
Tears dribble down his face sticky
as phlegm. His silent groaning shakes
his body, quivering with an angry terror.
He knows no peace, not even while
he sleeps. Then, one morning, sudden
as doves waking to sing to the sun,
he opens his eyes, surprised to find,
like a visitor from across far seas unlearned
in a people's speech, he can speak in
the simplest ways the rudiments of their language.

4.

He had long ago deserted his home,
its gardens weed-infested,
thunder clouds hovering over
the village in November,
night reclaiming the last pale
slip of a sun, rows of bushes
he had neglected bent toward
the ground. Now, as each day grows
shorter, colder, snow flurries whiter
than the pillow where he lays
his head, he recalls the woods
in his early boyhood whose joy
in spring perplexed him with the freedom
of bare-fanged wolf, wild boar, black feathered grouse.

5.

On a starless night, he composes
crazed music. The emperor
is half-mad, his court even madder.
Near him, people die while still crying.
A chill wind frosts every garden.
An invisible wind is echoing
the sense of the sky. His soul feels
mad too, sometimes, crazed by
unspeakable longings. A raven caws on
a snowy night. He sings alone.
If it must be so, so be it.
An ill-lit sky is indifferent
to a humanity that lodges in rooms
by the side of a road it hastens to depart on tomorrow.

6.

Sailing on shifting breezes, snakeskin-thin clouds
stretch and dissolve into the sky over the hills.

At the edge of a forest, a shallow stream eddies
in the shade of weeping willows and tall black pine.

A friend who has grown distant over time reminds
him of the happier years they led before they knew fear.

A man who holds back his feelings might still burn
like sunset tangled in trees on autumn evenings.

During an afternoon thunder shower, the rain sounds
heavy as leaves falling after they've lost their grip.

If he cannot accept that God is real, a meadow's yellow
grass and browning flowers, why allow himself to dream?

Young, he'd tromped a branch-broken trail on a mountain
side, picked widespread, dandelion, hazelnut, black elder.

Gusts scattered white laurel clusters, bachelor's buttons,
love-in-the-mist, oleander while he listened to the cuckoo.

Now nights grow chill, days stranger and more distant, like you,
always changing, always in the world somewhere, shining, his beloved.

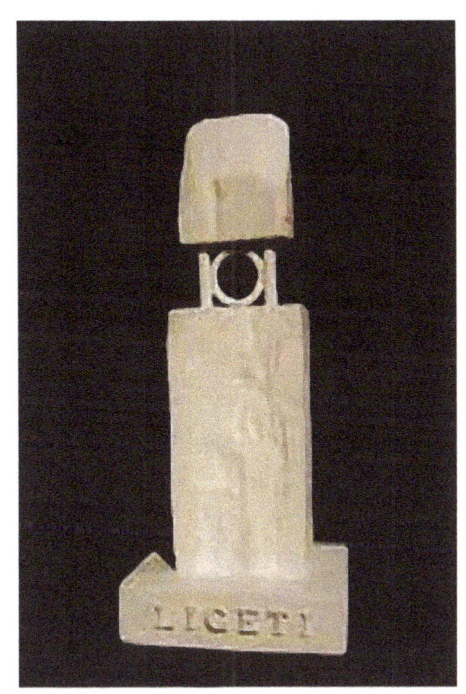

LIGETI

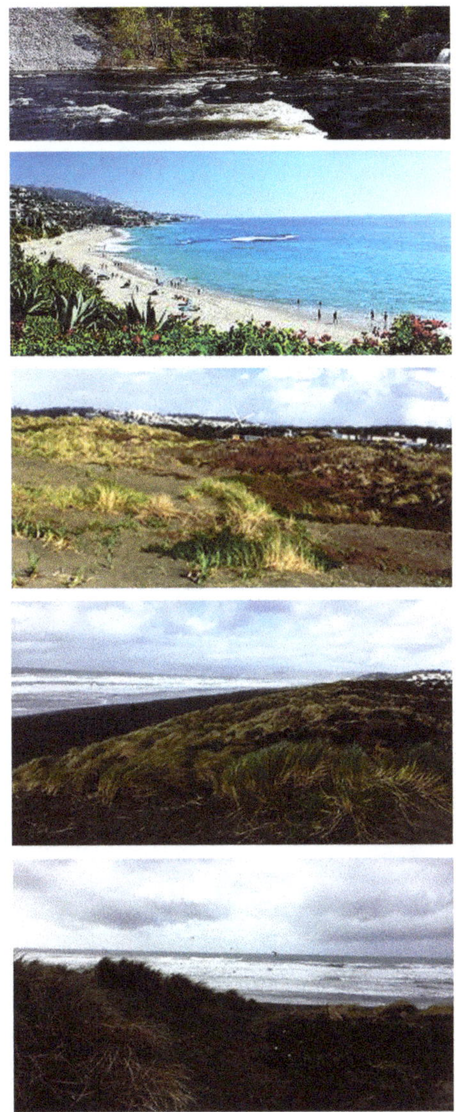